THE GREAT I AM

Preaching The "I Am" Statements Of Jesus

RONALD J. LAVIN

CSS Publishing Company, Inc.
Lima, Ohio

THE GREAT I AM

Copyright © 1995 by
CSS Publishing Company, Inc.
Lima, Ohio

Library of Congress Cataloging-in-Publication Data

Lavin, Ronald J.
    The great I am : preaching the "I am" statements of Jesus / Ronald J. Lavin.
      p.   cm.
    Includes bibliographical references.
    ISBN 0-7880-0576-6
    1. Jesus Christ—Divinity—Sermons. 2. God—Name—Sermons. 3. Bible. N.T. John—Sermons. 4. Bible. N.T. Revelation—Sermons. 5. Lutheran Church—Sermons. 6. Sermons, English. I. Title.
BT216.L38
231—dc20   95-12244
                                                      CIP

This book is available in the following formats, listed by ISBN:
0-7880-0576-6 Book
0-7880-0577-4 IBM 3 1/2 computer disk
0-7880-0578-2 IBM 3 1/2 book and disk package
0-7880-0579-0 Macintosh computer disk
0-7880-0580-4 Macintosh book and disk package
0-7880-0581-2 IBM 5 1/4 computer disk
0-7880-0582-0 IBM 5 1/4 book and disk package

PRINTED IN U.S.A.

GREAT
AMERICAN

PREACHER
SERIES

The Great American Preacher Series epitomizes the kind of quality writing, scholarship and practicality which have shaped the foundation of CSS preaching resources for nearly three decades.

Written by some of America's best contemporary preachers, this series promises to inspire you with fresh insights into the timeless message of the Gospel; provide models of excellence for sermon creation; deal respectfully and sensitively with the Word of God; spark your own imagination and creativity with outline and illustration possibilities; and minister to you personally as you continue to grow in your relationship with God and others.

CSS Publishing Company considers it a privilege to be a part of your preaching, study and reading disciplines. With additional volumes planned in the future, we invite you to become a regular participant in this adventure of shared ideas.

This book is dedicated to my mother Alma Lavin,
who first pointed me to the Great I AM by her love.

Table Of Contents

Preface

Why write a book on the I AM sayings in the Bible? Why focus on the name of God when so many in our churches seem content to focus on those elements in Christianity which focus on how we might feel more fulfilled and have better relations with other people? Precisely because the I AM of the Bible is a corrective for a this-sided religion, this emphasis on God, the transcendent One, is needed.

Chapter one, "The Great I AM," focuses on the problem which this book repeatedly addresses by describing our society as "a push-button society" where people think they are in control, just like they control their television sets with electronic buttons. The continuing, ongoing problem for people in every age is idolatry, having gods created by human hands which we control, instead of the one true God. The last chapter, "I Am Coming Soon," is on the same subject, but is placed entirely in narrative form in the hope that you, the reader, will not just get into the text but have the text and the theme of God's ultimate control get into you.

Two chapters deal with the "I AM" sayings in a context outside God's name. "I am coming soon" (chapter 14) is not God's proper name, but what God in Christ is doing and will do in establishing his lordship over us. "I am making all things new" (chapter 11) is not God's proper name, but the activity of God in Christ on the cross doing for us what we cannot do for ourselves. God controls things from a throne called the cross.

God is in control. Not you. Not me. God. Religions which get caught up in a this-sided horizontal emphasis greatly endanger the biblical emphasis that God is over us and will one day judge us.

We may be caught in self-deception about ourselves and illusions about God, but the GREAT I AM is not mocked. What we sow, we shall reap. The biblical corrective for self-centered Americans is the focus on the vertical dimension of being a Christian. Jesus is Lord and he is coming soon. The Holy Spirit is calling, guiding and directing us. Are we paying attention?

This book is addressed to laity and pastors. The questions of this book are not speculative but practical: What shall I believe? Who is over me? What shall I do? If God is the GREAT I AM, Jesus the Lord is coming soon, and the Holy Spirit is guiding us, what does that mean for my faith-in-action today? What difference does it make that God is the GREAT I AM?

Questions at the end of each chapter are intended for group discussion about the difference faith in action makes today. This book may, of course, be used for individual guidance, but it is best used for enrichment and discussion in Bible classes or small groups. Repeatedly, we need to ask questions like these: Who is this GREAT I AM? What does it mean that I am under the control of the Lord? How is the Holy Spirit guiding my life?

Instead of standing in the middle asking the questions, we must listen to the questions raised by the GREAT I AM. In the Jewish tradition, the one in control asks the questions. I AM is asking us questions in the Bible verses in this book. Are we listening?

Special appreciation goes to Kathy Shutt of Huntington Beach, California, who typed the final draft of this book, and to Pat Weber of Tucson, Arizona, who typed early versions of the chapters. Kathy and Pat added clarity where it was lacking. Where clarity is still lacking, I am responsible.

In addition, appreciation goes to King of Glory Lutheran Church in Fountain Valley, California, where I am the Senior Pastor, and to my wife Joyce, my partner in ministry. Time has been provided for me to write, a ministry which I believe God has given me.

Theological Prologue

With a theme like I AM, this book is about the transcendence of God. While God's transcendence needs to be emphasized, the second side of the paradox, God's immanence, is not overlooked. The GREAT I AM was incarnated in the person of Jesus Christ. The paradox is that Jesus is both divine and human, celebrating the mystery of the incarnation, and avoiding the heresy of both docetism (Jesus was not really divine) and modalism (Jesus was a mode of God and not really human).

While the divine side of Jesus is the biblical corrective for a generation caught up in itself and wanting to avoid a God of judgment, the human side of Jesus helps us to know God because God knows what we are going through. While the Trinity of confessional Christianity is the substructure of this book, the focus of this book is Jesus and his I AM statements. While the human side of Jesus is a part of the Trinitarian substructure of this book, the divinity of Jesus is the theme.

There are dangers in writing a book on the I AM sayings of the Bible. One danger is that in focusing on the divinity of Christ as revealed in his I AM statements we can minimize his humanity and thus push to the edges the doctrine of the Trinity, firmly fixed as it is on the incarnation, crucifixion, and resurrection of Jesus and the giving of the Holy Spirit of God to the church for mission. Quite the opposite is my intention.

"I AM WHO I AM" is God's proper name. Jesus uses the name I AM for himself to show his divinity, not to the exclusion of his humanity, but in addition to his humanity. Paul puts it this way. "God was in Christ reconciling the world unto himself..." (2 Corinthians 5:19). Jesus' suffering, death, and resurrection give life to us.

If the Spirit of him who raised Jesus from the dead dwells in you, he who raised Christ from the dead will give life to your mortal bodies also through his Spirit that dwells in you.
—Romans 8:11 (NRSV)

11

By emphasizing any of the sayings of Jesus in a book, including the "I AM" sayings, there is no intention to minimize the saving work of the Son of God on the cross and the mission inspired by the Holy Spirit to empower the people of God for mission. Quite the contrary! The One who used the I AM name for himself is the One who so identified with our sins that nothing short of his death would atone for them.

The One who said, "Before Abraham was, I am," implying that people did not know who he was, is the same One who said, "Father, forgive them, for they don't know what they do," stating that people did not know what he was doing by his sacrificial death on the cross. The humiliation of the cross is not being overlooked as we look at the glorification of the I AM sayings of the Lord. The theology of the cross is the heart of the matter as we examine the theology and practical implications of Jesus who used the I AM name for himself.

By looking at the I AM sayings of Jesus, we don't get the whole picture, but we can get a helpful corrective for a "this-sided" popularization of Christianity which makes Jesus into little more than another human teacher. Chapter eight deals with the paradox of Jesus' humanity *and* divinity, the heart of our Trinitarian baptismal formula, "In the name of the Father and of the Son and of the Holy Spirit." The Trinity is not being pushed to the sidelines by the focus on the I AM sayings of Jesus in the Bible stories we examine here. One aspect of this formula is being examined in order to better understand the whole message. Hopefully, we will better understand who God is as we look at what God does in the stories in this book.

1

The Great I AM

But Moses said to God, "If I come to the Israelites and say to them, 'The God of your ancestors has sent me to you,' and they ask me, 'What is his name?' what shall I say to them?" God said to Moses, "I AM WHO I AM." He said further, "Thus you shall say to the Israelites, 'I AM has sent me to you.'" God also said to Moses, "Thus you shall say to the Israelites, 'The LORD, the God of your ancestors, the God of Abraham, the God of Isaac, and the God of Jacob, has sent me to you':

This is my name forever,
and this my title for all
generations."
— Exodus 3:13-15 (NRSV)

"Before Abraham was, I AM."
— John 8:58 (NRSV)

At a recent retreat for pastors, one of the presenters, Rick Melheim from the Lutheran Leadership Institute in St. Paul, Minnesota, said something which really describes our times:

*We live in a **push-button society**. We have the control panel in our hands. When we don't like what is on the television, we push a button and change the station. We are in control. That makes for a very distorted picture of reality. We think that we can control everything.*

It's true. We can push a button and change stations. We control what we will see and hear from a control panel which gives us a distorted view of life. If we don't like something, "click, click," and it's on to another station.

In addition, many modern people can control their VCRs and their tape decks in much the same way. "Click, click," and the things we see and hear change, at our command. Some people live in gated communities. "Click, click," and the gate opens at the flick of a thumb. Some people even have automatic house door openers, and car door openers.

One man said he has a control panel which operates six functions in his home. That's power. It gives us the feeling, "I am in charge." That's the problem! That's the lie.

The biblical corrective for being the center of the universe is contained in our texts which insist that "THE GREAT I AM" is in charge. God told Moses that his name is I AM. Jesus said, "Before Abraham was, I AM."

The Push-Button Society

"I Am In Charge"

Button, button, who's got the button? "I have it and I'm going to keep it," we reply.

During Lent, Christians think about Jesus' life, suffering, and his death. We also think about our lives. On Ash Wednesday we have ashes placed on our foreheads as a sign that we are limited creatures who have sinned, people who need a Savior. We are signed with the sign of the cross and we hear these words as the ashes are placed on our foreheads:

Remember your mortality.
Anticipate your eternity.

Button, button, who's got the button? To remember our mortality means to confess that we are not in charge. Our greatest sin is

14

to stand in the middle and think that we are in charge and that like spokes in a wheel, everything revolves around us.

Button, button, who's got the button? We forget to remember that we are creatures, not the Creator. We forget to remember that we have limits and that one of those limits is that we were never intended to stand in the middle. We forget to remember our mortality. Along comes Ash Wednesday and the ashes remind us to remember. "You come from ashes, to ashes you will return." We stop and remember our mortality.

Button, button, who's got the button? "Not me," we reply in confession. "My life is out of control when I hold the control panel and change the stations as I desire. It doesn't work for me to be at the control panel." "Yes," says God in reply to our confession. "I know. I made you that way. You were never intended to be in charge."

Button, button, who's got the button? "You do," we say to God when we receive the ashes for remembering. "You, O Lord, have the control panel. My life is broken and dysfunctional unless you are the One who rules." God replies, "Remember your mortality, my son, my daughter. Now you are in touch with me. Anticipate your eternity. I AM in charge."

The Kingdom Of God

"I AM" Is In Charge

Button, button, who's got the button? "You have it, O King of the Universe. Only you are the great I AM."

Enter Moses. Behold a burning bush on the mountain near Midian. Listen to the voice of God. "Take off your shoes. The ground on which you stand is holy ground."

It was the custom in Eastern countries that to show reverence, shoes were taken off when a person went to a holy place. Moses did as he was told. Moses then entered into dialogue with the living God. God said to Moses, "Moses, go down to Egypt." Moses said to God, "I cannot go." God said to Moses, "Moses, I'll go with you." Moses said to God, "I cannot go." God said to

15

Moses, "Moses, you will be my spokesman." But again, Moses objected. He said, "I am not eloquent." God said, "Moses, I made your tongue." Moses said, "I know, but I am still afraid." On and on went the debate, until God finally promised that he would send Moses' brother Aaron to be a spokesman for him. Moses finally agreed, but before he went Moses asked: "What name shall I give when the people ask, 'Who sent you?'" Moses was asking for the name of God. God gave him this name: "Tell them 'I AM WHO I AM' sent you."

God was telling Moses that he is the one who has no beginning and no ending, the Alpha and the Omega, the A and the Z, the beginning and the end of all things. God is the One from whom all things come, and the One to whom all things go. Remember this name: "THE GREAT I AM."

THE GREAT I AM is the One in control. When we give up the push-button control panel to God we discover that our lives work. There is power in this name: I AM.

It is time to give up control to God. It is not easy to give up control, but it is necessary. It's the one thing needful and the hardest thing of all. Submission replaces rebellion with no little conflict.

Enter Jesus. Conflict comes in the presence of the I AM. Read the eighth chapter of the Gospel of John. It is filled with conflict. The chapter opens with the story of the woman caught in adultery. It's a trap set by Jesus' enemies. "Tell us, should we stone her or set her free?" they ask. If Jesus says, "Stone her," they will reply, "We thought you taught mercy and forgiveness." If Jesus says, "Set her free," they will reply, "Are you above the law of Moses which teaches that a woman caught in adultery should be stoned?" A perfect trap, or so it seems. Jesus writes in the sand. What does he write? Perhaps the names of the men who had stones in their hands. Then Jesus looks up. He looks into the eyes of the trembling woman. He looks into the eyes of the accusers. "Let him who is without sin cast the first stone," he says. Sinners quietly drop their stones and depart. The great reversal. Conflict. Tension. But it's only the beginning. "Has no one condemned you?" Jesus says to the adulterous woman. Her bottom lip is trembling with fear. "No one," she says. "Neither do I condemn you," he replies. Submission leads to freedom, but not without conflict and tension.

More conflict and tension comes with verse 12. "I AM the light of the world," Jesus says. There is *that name* I AM again, God's name. Jesus is using it for himself. Conflict and tension. Are you testifying on your own behalf? Are you bragging, using God's holy name for yourself? The conflict and tension rise a notch, but go on and read the rest of the chapter. You haven't seen anything yet. Submission is not easy for the proud and arrogant religious leaders.

Let's pick up the story in verse 24. Jesus says, "You will die in your sins unless you believe in me" (8:24). "Just who do you think you are? How can you, an itinerant nobody, tell us that we are going to hell?" The conflict goes up a notch.

Now look at verse 31. The conversation about Abraham gets hot. The volume on the conflict is shouting level, "God's true children, the real children of Abraham, would hear God's Word," Jesus says. "You are not Abraham's children. You just don't get it."

Can you turn up the volume above a yelling and screaming level? That's where the religious leaders are. They are in a rage. That brings us to Jesus' calm, soft, poignant resolution, which encourages them even more. "Are you greater than our father Abraham?" they cry out cynically (8:57). Quietly, but with a resonance which cannot be missed, Jesus boldly steps up the conflict to the ultimate level: **"Very truly, I tell you, before Abraham was I AM."**

The ultimate insult! I AM is God's name: Rage turns to physical violence. They pick up stones to throw at him, just like some of these same people had picked up stones to throw at the woman caught in adultery at the beginning of chapter eight.

But Jesus slips out of the temple before they can put him to death.

Button, button, who's got the button? That's what this chapter is all about. Jesus through word, deed, and name has the control button.

Almost a century ago, Adelaide Pollard was at the end of her rope. She was terribly discouraged and depressed. She had been trying to raise funds to underwrite the cost of a long voyage to Africa where she planned to work as a missionary. Her efforts left her far short of her goal and she wondered "Why doesn't God help me when I'm trying to do his work?" In desperation she went to a prayer meeting at a local church, but her spirits were so low, she couldn't take part.

An older woman in the group prayed first and Adelaide was surprised by what she heard. Instead of the usual petitions for blessings in the form of improved health, the safety of her loved ones or food upon their table, the woman simply prayed: "Lord, it really doesn't matter what You do with us — just have Your way with our lives." Adelaide was stunned when she realized that by contrast, she was practically *telling* God what he *must do* to make *her* dream of missionary work a reality!

She went home in silence and opened her Bible to the 18th chapter of Jeremiah:

> *The word that came to Jeremiah from the Lord, "Come, go down to the potter's house and there I will let you hear my words." So I went down to the potter's house and there he was working at his wheel. The vessel he was making of clay was spoiled in the potter's hand, and he reworked it into another vessel, as seemed good to him. Then the word of the Lord came to me, "Can I not do with you, O House of Israel, just as this potter has done? Just like the clay in the potter's hand, so are you in my hand, O House of Israel."*
>
> — Jeremiah 18:1-6 (NRSV)

That same evening Adelaide Pollard composed the words to a well-known hymn which has inspired countless believers the past century:

> *Have Thine own way, Lord, have Thine own way.*
> *Thou art the potter, I am the clay.*
> *Mold me and make me after Thy will*
> *While I am waiting — yielded still.*

18

Button, button, who's got the button? God. God is THE GREAT I AM, and we are his creatures.

God has the button. When I hold it and change stations and try to control things so that I will be satisfied and entertained, everything goes out of control.

"Thou art the potter. I am the clay." The One who understands you is standing with you. The One in control wants only the best for you. Jesus showed us what the I AM is like. Once we get this straight, we can pray the prayer Jesus taught us, "Our Father..."

Behold, THE GREAT I AM, who created the heavens and the earth, is your "Abba," your daddy.

Questions For
Reflection Or Discussion

1. How many push-button controls do you have at your house?

2. What do they open, close, change?

3. What's so wrong with "a push-button society"?

4. Why was Moses so reluctant to go for God?

5. Why are we so reluctant to serve?

6. How do the words, "Have Your Own Way," affect you personally?

7. In what areas?

2

I Am The Light Of The World

"I am the light of the world."
— John 8:12 (NRSV)

"As long as I am in the world, I am the light of the world."
— John 9:5 (NRSV)

"You are the light of the world. A city built on a hill cannot be hid. No one after lighting a lamp puts it under the bushel basket, but on the lampstand, and it gives light to all in the house. In the same way, let your light shine before others, so that they may see your good works, and give glory to your Father in heaven."
— Matthew 5:14-16 (NRSV)

Imagine that you are in a very dark place, where you cannot see. In the darkest places, you would not be as much in the dark as the blind man described in the ninth chapter of the Gospel of John, but imagining yourself in a dark room may help you get into the story in which Jesus says, "I am the light of the world."

Actually, the blindness described in the text is two-fold: the physical blindness of the man and the spiritual blindness of the Pharisees (John 8:13-19). It is the latter about which we should most concern ourselves, since spiritual blindness remains a serious problem for many — for people both in the church and outside the church. Jesus came to be the light of the world. That is a needed message for those who dwell in spiritual darkness.

Imagine The Possibilities When Jesus Is Our Light

Jesus came bringing light to our darkness in order that we might see better and that we might help others see better. A line from the play *Butterflies Are Free* describes the problem of spiritual blindness well: "There are none so blind as those who refuse to see." That's the Pharisees' problem. They aren't physically blind, yet they do not see. They are not paying attention.

An old nursery rhyme describes the blindness of those who refuse to see:

> *Pussy cat, pussy cat, where have you been?*
> *I've been to London to visit the Queen.*
> *Pussy cat, pussy cat, what did you there?*
> *I frightened a mouse under the chair.*

The cat didn't see the Queen or the castle or London. The cat only saw the mouse. There is a blindness in that cat. We see only what gets our attention. That blindness is identified in Isaiah 42:20: "You have seen many things, but have paid no attention" (NIV).

Please note that it isn't physical blindness but not paying attention to what is seen, which is the problem. "What gets your attention, gets you," E. Stanley Jones once said. If you give your attention to sin and glance at God, sin will get you. If you give your attention to God and glance at sin, God will get you. Spiritual blindness consists of giving our attention to something other than God.

An ineffective pastor was once described to me in these terms: "He majors in minors." In other words, he did not make the most of his time. To live as "children of light" (Ephesians 5:8), we are called to "make the most of the time" (Ephesians 5:16). Anything less is spiritual blindness, "refusing to see."

Jesus is the light of the world. He shines in the darkness like a laser beam knifing its way through a dark night, or like a beacon light on the black sea. He shines in the darkness like the sun which came up behind me as I traveled on a highway recently in the foggy, bleak and dark morning. That sun radiated out a new warmth and light which changed my attitude about the whole day. Jesus is like that. Jesus is the light of the world, and that new light means new life, as the Gospel of John says. In the opening chapter of the Gospel of John, we read these words: "In him (that is in Jesus) was life and that life was the light of men" (John 1:4 NRSV).

A friend recently wrote,

> *The weather outside has a lot to do with how I feel inside. Today I felt down and realized that I felt that way because it was dark and gloomy outside. I feel so fantastic when its sunny outside. It's the same way with Jesus in your life. He gives you light; brings you out of the 'gloomy' life and lifestyle. He opens your eyes and lets you see what is really important in life and gives you a purpose for really living.*

Many people claim that the kind of day it is has a lot to do with their mood. If it is a dark, gloomy day, they tend to feel dark and gloomy. On a bright, sunny day they tend to feel bright and sunny. If that is true for you, then I hope you will remember that Jesus is the very warming rays of God which come to our dark world in order to change our attitude. Jesus is a mood changer. Through an attitude change, he can help you interpret what is happening around you in a new and different way. Jesus said, "I am the light of the world."

The first chapter of the Gospel of John tells us that there is something about Jesus' light, that he had a quality of eternal life in him which gave light to other people. The Gospel says that that new quality of life was something that helped people see better, not in the physical sense, but in the sense that we would be able to perceive and know better what was going on in the world.

"In him was life and the life was the light of all people" (John 1:4, NRSV). That means that the life which is from God comes to this dark little planet and sheds new insight and new perception so that those who come to the Word of life can see better and know better and live better and be better. Imagine the possibilities.

Jesus said, "As long as I am in the world, I am the light of the world" (John 9:5, NRSV). He also said to the disciples, "You are the light of the world" (Matthew 5:14, NRSV). When you put these two verses together they mean that when Jesus is gone, he expects his disciples to continue the light of life which he brought. That's quite a job description!

Imagine The Possibilities When We Know That We Are The Light Of The World

On Wednesday, October 27, 1993, I walked to University of Arizona Hospital where I had a doctor's appointment. There I was greeted by a large United Way sign at the entrance: "IMAGINE THE POSSIBILITIES." That made me stop and think about the Word of God and our lives. Imagine the possibilities if Christians start using the light God gives them.

Dr. Reuel Howe, the author of *The Miracle Of Dialogue*, told me that one of his most meaningful meditations is to imagine that the inhaling of air is the inhaling of light and the exhaling of air from his body is the exhaling of darkness. In doing this spiritual exercise, Dr. Howe said he was amazed one day to discover that he had exhaled the darkness out of himself while inhaling the light and that he felt that he had truly come to be a "little Christ" for God. God had cast out the darkness in him and was, therefore, making him an effective instrument. He didn't mean that he was a perfect instrument, or that he had no darkness in himself, but only that as he felt the light of God was taking over his life, he himself could shine more brightly in the world. That is a good story for all of us. We need to be breathing in the light of God and the life of God, and exhaling the darkness and the demonic powers within us. As we do so, we are not only happier and better integrated as persons, but more effective witnesses for God. We need vision to help others find the light of life. Imagine the possibilities.

Being in the dark, either physically or spiritually, is like being in prison. In the beautiful autobiography *To Catch An Angel*, Robert Russell describes that prison for those who are physically blind. In one of the most moving scenes he tells how after getting a PhD in literature he was unable to secure a teaching job because of his blindness and how going back to the workshop for the blind, though it was a blessing in some ways, was, in some ways, like going back to prison.

24

Worst of all was being reminded of the shame—not the shame of defeat, but the deep and insidious shame of blindness. Being forced back into the workshop was to be reminded all over again of my inadequacy, all over again to clench my fists in impotent rage, to feel all over again the hot tears scald my cheeks. It was this shame I had yearned to escape from while I was at the Institute, and which the system of segregation so tragically reinforced. It was this of which my life during the last ten years had been so blessedly free — exorcised by friendship and love.

Escape it he did. This blind man learned to live on a river and even go fishing. He writes:

So that I can go out by myself whenever I please, I have run a wire down to the end of the dock, where I have mounted a large electric bell. Before I go down to the dock, I plug the line into an outlet in the house. A timing device permits the bell to ring only once every thirty seconds. If I row too far upwind to be able to hear the bell, I can still fish without anxiety because I can always drift downwind, and then I am again in touch with my base.

And a man needs a base to quest from, and he needs the sense that, however far he has strayed, return is still possible. Confidence that he has such a base is all that gives him the courage to reach past the edges of the familiar. It may be what he knows, what he believes, the table round, or heaven itself. The river lies before me, a constant invitation, a constant challenge, and my bell is the thread of sound along which I return.

To a quiet base.

Jesus came to free us from the prison of spiritual darkness and to use us to free others by leading them to the kingdom of light and life. We are called to be fishers of men. Imagine the possibilities.

25

In a society of specialists where we know more and more about less and less, we tend to lose sight of the bigger picture. People get engrossed in their work, or their schooling, or their families — all good things, but not if they mean losing sight of God. This is the potential spiritual blindness described by Isaiah as "not paying attention."

One man has written:

> *Some people cannot see and do not behold.*
> *This is called blindness.*
> *Some people cannot see even though they behold.*
> *This is called physical sight.*
> *Some people see beyond what they behold.*
> *This is called vision.*

(Anonymous)

God, give us vision that we may help others see, that our witness may be effective. Everyone can be an angel of light, no matter how old they are. Imagine the possibilities.

Victoria ("Torrie") Schlecht is four years old. I baptized her soon after she was born. At a communion service, I knelt down to bless Torrie, as we do for all the little children. As I made the sign of the cross on her forehead and said, "Remember, Jesus loves you very much," a light dawned behind her eyes, she smiled and suddenly put out her hand and made the sign of the cross on my forehead. A shiver ran up and down my spine.

I had been under a lot of tension, due to a move from Tucson, Arizona to Fountain Valley, California. A voice deep from within said silently, "Thanks, Torrie, my little angel of Light. I needed that."

There is a beautiful stanza in a folk song about light which puts it all together for me:

> *And Jesus said,*
> *I am the light of the world.*
> *You people come and follow me.*
> *If you follow in love,*

26

You'll learn the mystery
Of what you can do and you can be.

We are called to shine like lights in the world. We cannot do that unless we continually return to the Lord who is the light of the world. We must breathe in the light before we can exhale the light We must go home, before we can go out. We must return to the quiet base before we can go out on the river of life.

We are called to pay attention and listen for the bell of God tolling like a church bell in a quiet town, calling us to return home to God. Do not ask "for whom the bell tolls. It tolls for you."

Imagine the possibilities.

Questions For
Reflection Or Discussion

1. What experiences have you had with light and darkness?

2. Have you ever seen a lighthouse in the dark on the sea? Describe it.

3. Have you ever been away from man-made light with only flashlight to guide you? How did it feel?

4. As a child, were you ever lost? How did it feel?

5. What connections do your experiences have with Jesus' word "I AM the light of the world"?

6. In what ways can we Christians be lights in the dark world for others?

3

I Am The Way, The Truth, And The Life

Simon Peter said, "Lord, we do not know where you are going"...Thomas said, "Lord, we do not know where you are going, so how can we know the way?" Jesus said, "I am the Way, the Truth, and the Life."
— John 13:36—14:6 (J.B.)

Have you ever gotten lost or felt anxious because of the absence of someone on whom you depended? That's what the apostles felt one day, shortly before the death of Jesus, as the Master talked with them in the upper room where the Lord's supper was instituted.

The apostles were like children who had wandered away from a parent in a large crowd. Confusion and anxiety resulted from Jesus speaking about leaving them. "Where are you going?" Peter asked.

In answer to Simon Peter, Jesus said, "I am going to my Father." In answer to Thomas who asked, "How do we know the way to the Father?" Jesus answered, "I am the Way...to the Father." He added, "I am also the Truth (which sets free — John 8:32) and the Life (which enables action — John 3:21).

This saying, "I am the Way," gave rise to the earliest name by which Christians were known — "followers of the Way." Christians are followers of the Way. They are not the Way; they claim absoluteness for Jesus, not Christianity. Followers of Jesus point beyond themselves to him. He is the way.

The Way to what? The Way to the Father! Jesus gives us access to the Father. Shakespeare, although he can show me a way to write poetry, is not himself the way for me to write poetry. Michelangelo, although he can show me a good way to paint, is not himself the way to painting. Saint Peter, although he can show me a way to draw close to God, is himself not the Way. Jesus is the Way. He not only walked the way, he is the Way; Jesus is the One who knows from whence he came and where he is going. Jesus gladly shows us where he has been and where he is going. Since we have a tendency to get lost or stranded, it is good to know that we have a guide on the way.

The Christian life can be described as getting on the way and staying on the way.

Getting On The Way

Many of us got on the Way to eternal life as babies through Holy Baptism. I don't remember it, of course, but my mother told me that she took me to a Roman Catholic church in Chicago one Sunday afternoon shortly after I was born. There I was baptized and began the Christian life. I was "baptized into Christ" as Paul says. It was like starting a long journey.

It was not until 18 years later, after I had wandered away from the Way, that I saw the Way clearly and said, "I know that's the Way I am supposed to go." My commitment to walk that Way was an important step in the journey. As Christ was the central figure in baptism, so he was the central figure in the commitment which I made at age 18. I certainly would not have made a commitment to the church. I believed that it was full of hypocrites. I couldn't make a commitment to God as I knew him then, because he seemed too far away and distant. But Christ was real to me. I read about him in the Gospels and I sensed his presence as One who understood me and affirmed me. Had Jesus been a goal toward which I strove, I could not have reached him. He met me where I was, away from the road, and showed me where the road was. He also stayed with me on the road as a guide.

Jesus is the Way. A poem puts it this way:

Thou are the Way.
Hadst Thou been nothing but the goal,
I cannot say
If thou hadst ever met my soul.

— Alice Meynell

We do not need to reach God as the end of our striving. Jesus puts an end to our frustrated striving to reach God. As Paul writes, "It is not a matter of achieving, but believing..." (Romans 3:27, Phillips translation). It is a matter of trusting Jesus who is one with the Father (John 14:10).

Other ways to reach God do not work. For example, the way of hedonism is a dead-end street. Hedonism is the philosophy of pleasure. I saw this philosophy expressed on a bumper sticker recently: "If it feels good, do it." In searching for the good life through pleasure, the hedonist is really searching for God. The "eat, drink, and be merry" way of life that many try is an attempt at ultimate happiness, a happiness which can only be found in God. The philosophy of sexual liberation which we see all around us in the movies, television, and books is a search for fulfillment which ends in despair. Hedonism is a dead-end street because sex and pleasure, while good, were never intended to be ultimate.

So is humanism. Humanism may be defined as a philosophy of life centered in human effort. Unlike the hedonist, the humanist will frequently center many of his energies on giving pleasure to others instead of just seeking pleasure for himself. Unlike the hedonist, the humanist will generally try to be moral and concerned about what is right. Unlike the hedonist who is free-wheeling and self-centered, the humanist will frequently be uptight because he will have repressed many of his natural feelings for what is considered the greater good. But like the hedonist, the humanist at best considers God a distant point of reference. He will discover that he is on a dead-end way. He has no one to show him the way. He, too, will be lost on the long journey of life.

Frequently, the humanist will center much of his life on reason. He will live by ideas, many of them good ideas like "love your neighbor" and "keep the law," but he will not be able to maintain his walk through life based on reason because reason has its limits too. Jesus said, "I am the Truth," which means that ultimate reality is not a set of logical propositions, but a person. A life based on facts and logic isn't all bad, of course, because God made our minds, but it cannot bring us ultimate fulfillment because of the absence of the quality called faith or trust. That brings us to consideration of religion as a way.

But religion is a dead-end street too. Jesus never taught that religion would get us to God. Religion, as I'm using the term here, represents man's attempts to wrestle with the questions of life in reference to some kind of ultimate reality through some kind of faith or loyalty. Certainly no one would say that this attempt is all bad. The religious person, unlike the hedonist, is not only concerned about his own pleasures, but the happiness of others. Unlike the humanist, he has values beyond the human realm. But like both, he discovers that his way of religion does not fulfill his ultimate desire. At its best, religion is man's attempt to think about and live by some reference to God. The reason why no man-made religion works is because it is man-made. Religion is *not* the way to God.

Jesus never said religion is the way to God. He spoke of himself, not religion, as the Way. I wish I could introduce you in person to Jesus as a friend. He always had a way of helping people who had built barriers between themselves and God. He came to overcome those barriers. This young God in the garb of a nobody is our Way to personal fulfillment and relationship with God.

Jesus said, "I am the Way, the Truth, and the Life." You were made by his hand. "All things were made through him and nothing was made without him," the Gospel of John says. You will one day return to him. "I am the Alpha and the Omega, the beginning and the end," Jesus said. The only way we get onto the road that leads to eternity is through him. And the only way we stay on that road is also through him.

Staying On The Way

Once we are awakened to the limited nature of every other

philosophy, we may be awakened to the eternal nature of Christ and our call to follow him. Thus awakened, we may start out with some hesitation walking the Christian way. These first steps of walking the Way of Christ are like the first steps we took when we started to walk as babies. We stumble and fall. We bruise ourselves. We need assistance. At times we go back to what appears to be "an easier way," only to realize that the "easier way" doesn't get us anywhere.

It is one thing to begin our walk with Christ. It is quite another to stay on that walk with him. That was the problem which the Apostles experienced. They had begun their walk with God through Christ. When he told them that he was going away, they did not know how they could continue the Christian walk without him. What they didn't remember was that the living Christ would return in the form of the Holy Spirit. The apostles felt lost and stranded.

Have you ever gotten lost on a trip? Have you ever been stranded? Both of these experiences have happened to me. As a little boy, I remember being lost in the Chicago Stadium while attending a sports show. It was frightening.

I also remember that back in 1972 when I took over the leadership of a tour group in Rome, Italy, we were stranded for what seemed like days in the Rome airport. Being stranded gave me a terrible feeling of helplessness. In the journey of the Christian, sometimes a feeling of being lost or stranded can lead us away from the Way we should be going. That's why commitment to walk the true Way is so important.

The first step toward the kingdom of God is awakening to the dead-end nature of every other walk; the second is to commit ourselves to the long walk before us. This commitment is not a once and for all decision. It must be made and remade hundreds of times throughout a lifetime.

That's one of the reasons why I love old Christians so much. Like all of us, they have temptations to leave. Like all of us, they are disappointed when things don't work out well on the journey, when there is a fellow traveler who is a phony or a sickness or death of a loved one which is hard to understand. But the old Christian is someone who has stayed on the road through all of the temptations and disappointments, or more accurately, one who has returned to the Way, even when he has been overcome by disappointments. Old Christians have had to come back to the Way many times. They are an inspiration to all of us because we all know how easy it is to get off the Way onto side roads leading nowhere.

Dr. Sam Shoemaker helped many people get on the way and stay on the way. He summarized his life as standing by the door to the Way. He said that he was very concerned not to go too far into this Way because he was afraid that then he would forget those who are outside, but he was equally concerned that he not stay too far out, lest he leave the Way. He spoke of standing right at the most important door of all — the door to God — so that he could help others find the door, put their hand on the latch and go into the Way. He spoke of standing at the door to help those who become frightened and start out away from God. The people who are deep inside terrify some frightened people because they seem so pious and holy. Dr. Shoemaker, who helped many find the Way and many stay on the Way, was one of the prime movers of the small group movement in the twentieth century. He knew that it was not possible to travel the Way alone, that we need traveling companions. He started koinonia (fellowship) groups in the churches where he was pastor and he encouraged others to join in these study and prayer groups. "Dr. Sam," as he was affectionately called, was one of the founders of Alcoholics Anonymous, the best organization I know about to help alcoholics get back on the road to the good life.

One of the basic principles of Alcoholics Anonymous is that we need fellowship in order to stay on the right path. That's also one of the principles of Christianity. In fact, that is why Jesus created the Church. We need other Christians in this walk through life. We cannot stay on the Way alone.

In the person of Jesus, our guide, and in other Christians who travel with us, we sense the eternal life toward which we are moving. Both our guide and our group give us the encouragement to go on toward that life. We encourage others to move toward eternal life. Jesus is Life. His followers reflect that quality of life called eternal.

When you feel lost or stranded on your way through life, recall the words of the One who is the Way, the Truth, and the Life: "Don't let your hearts be troubled. Trust in God still, and trust in me..." It is as if he says, "I know where I'm going. I've walked this way before."

Jesus goes before us as our guide. We go together as a group. We can therefore go forward confidently because we are following him and he knows where he is going.

Questions For
Reflection Or Discussion

1. Have you traveled on the wrong road as you traveled by car? What resulted?

2. Some people say about religions, "You travel your road; I'll travel mine. We are all going on different roads to the same destination." How is this true? How is it false?

3. "Hedonism and humanism are roads to nowhere." Do you agree or disagree? Why?

4. Is religion good or bad?

5. What is attractive about old Christians? Do you know some?

4

I Am The Good Shepherd

I am the good shepherd. — John 10:11 (NRSV)

These words of Jesus bring us into contact once again with the great I AM. Who is this good shepherd? The one who made heaven and earth, the one from whom we came and the one to whom we go.

The Great I AM

The situation seemed out of control. The woman was dying of cancer. She had nowhere else to turn. She had tried all the chemotherapy which had been prescribed. She had even traveled to Mexico for a new treatment that a friend had experienced. Nothing worked. She was told to prepare for death. Nothing more could be done.

The Lutheran chaplain in the hospital worked with the hospice team to make the woman as comfortable as possible. In ministering to her, he discovered that she had been a Lutheran many years ago. When he asked her about it, she said that faith had not been a reality to her in her entire adult life. "John (my husband) and I got so caught up in making a living that we just forgot all about church and God," she said sadly. John chimed in, "We made lots of money. What good does it do us now?"

"It's never too late to return to God," the kindly chaplain suggested. "God is always waiting." "No," said the woman. "It is too late for me. I've been away too long — 70 years, since I was 13. We've done too many things wrong." The chaplain looked deeply into the dying woman's eyes. "I'd like you to try to think about two things: the Lord's Prayer and the twenty-third psalm. I'll come back and see you tomorrow."

The next day when the chaplain entered the room, the woman said, "I've been thinking. I do remember parts of the prayer and the psalm. My mother taught them to me. Would you help me say them?" "Certainly," said the pastor. They prayed together slowly, "Our Father who art in heaven..."

"Wait," said the dying woman who was just skin and bones. "What does that mean? What does it mean that God is our father?"

The chaplain bent close down to the woman who had forgotten all that she knew about God. "That means that God cares for you," he said. "You may have forgotten him, but he has not forgotten you. It also means that he is strong. The heavenly Father is stronger than death itself."

"You mean that he can cure me?" the woman begged. "Yes," said the pastor, "but your cancer is so far along, perhaps you should prepare for the greater cure, the cure for death." "What's that?" "That's life everlasting."

The patient was growing too weak to speak. "I'll come back tomorrow," the chaplain said.

When he returned the next day, the patient seemed to be sleeping. He was about to leave when she said softly, "Pastor, I want to talk." They talked for what seemed like hours, though it was only fifteen minutes. They talked about when she was a girl, the church she had attended, her pastor and her mother, who was a believer. "Do you want to try the Lord's Prayer again?" the pastor asked. "Yes...no," she said. "What was the psalm you mentioned the other day?"

For the next three days, the chaplain came and explained the twenty-third psalm to her in as simple a way as he could. "The great God who can conquer death for you because he sent his Son to die on the cross, is the tender, forgiving, caring shepherd of your soul," he said.

The Great I AM Is The Good Shepherd

Day One

The chaplain began by saying that the twenty-third psalm

has comforted and assured the hospitalized and the grieving; inspired and comforted the lost and the lonely, and lifted the spirits of the depressed for hundreds of years.

He went on:

It has enriched the lives of all who have read it and memorized it. Even people who say, "I'm not very religious" generally know the twenty-third psalm. It is personal: "the Lord is *my* shepherd," and poignant: "Thou preparest a table before me in the presence of my enemies." Its imagery is strong — both of a good shepherd with his sheep and a master of ceremonies at a banqueting table.

In our urban living, we may have difficulty getting into the rich rural imagery of the twenty-third psalm, but the result of studying this psalm is certainly worth the effort. "The Lord is my shepherd" is a reminder of God's caring. We like sheep have all gone astray, but the Good Shepherd seeks us out, finds us, and returns us to the flock of God, just like an ancient shepherd in the fields sought out his straying sheep.

A shepherd knows his sheep. He knows what they can do and what they cannot do. He knows that a sheep is so dumb that it will not even take care of itself. It must be in a flock or it will die. It needs shepherding, caring, togetherness. A good shepherd meets the needs of his flock — and even the wants.

"I shall not want" is a magnificent testimony to the caring of the Good Shepherd. Not only our needs, but also our wants are met, as long as they are not in conflict with the purposes of our Shepherd. We can be an utterly satisfied flock of God.

One of our needs is for rest. "He makes me lie down in green pastures." We can work, play, romp, enjoy, struggle, eat, and in our activism, half forget the time-tested truth that rest and peace and quiet are essential to life. Many hospital patients have told me, "I needed this rest." Sheep need to lie down to digest

39

their food. We need to rest to digest all that we take in. We need green pastures — places of withdrawal and digestion.

Day Two

As the chaplain entered the room on the second day, the woman looked frightened. He tried to get her refocused on the twenty-third psalm by talking about fears.

One of our needs is for someone to understand our fears. "The still waters" are the spots where the shepherd can lead his sheep across the streams and rivers. Sheep are afraid of moving waters. A good shepherd does not command his flock to cross where their fears would bring panic. He leads them to the quiet waters where he gently stills their fears and helps them cross.

Still another need is for renewal. All of us get tired. All are at times discouraged. All need to be renewed, made new again. "Behold, I am making all things new," says the Lord (Revelation 21:5 NRSV). That's good news. Psalm 23 puts it in terms of restoring life from the God who over and over again provides the possibility of new beginnings for his people. Sometimes we need new beginnings because we are "cast down."

Sheep can be "cast down," turned over on their backs, unable to raise themselves up. They are pathetic and vulnerable when they are cast down. They need to be restored by a shepherd or they will die from exposure or from attack. People are like that too.

We need renewed life. "He restores my life." He gives life to my life. Life of itself can be lived at a physical, animal level. Food, sex, shelter are all necessities for living. But they aren't enough! We need "life" added to our lives. Jesus said, "I came to give you life, and that is abundance." An extra dimension is added to our lives when we follow the Good Shepherd. As we fail, as we sin, as we are "cast down," we need to be brought back and given life again. As we die, we need what we cannot achieve — life again. It is "life again" which the Good Shepherd gives.

"Wait," said the woman. "I've always said, 'When you are dead, that's it.' Do you mean that there is more?" "Yes," said the chaplain. "For those who believe in Jesus Christ, the Good Shepherd, there is eternal life. Let me tell you about what the psalmist meant by 'paths of righteousness.' "

We need to know the right paths along which to travel through life. Wrong paths include idolatry, immorality, wrong priorities, and the attractive distractions of the world, like money. All lead to our personal destruction.

We need right paths. "He leads me in the paths of righteousness" refers to right paths where dangers are lessened. God doesn't want us taking wrong paths where certain death awaits for us. The path of sexual passion brings sure death. The path of materialism brings sure death. The path of feeling sorry for ourselves brings sure death. God leads us in righteous paths.

Even taking the right path has its difficulties. While walking the right path, we must go through "the valley of the shadow of death," a valley where we must face the dangers of life and death, and must struggle to survive. Shadowy places are those wherein we cannot see our enemies very well. We need the shepherd's rod and staff to prod and guide us, even when we walk in the righteous paths wherein God leads.

"I've often walked on the wrong paths," the patient said. "Yes, but you can get back on the right path by simple faith," the pastor replied. "Let me tell you about God's rod and staff."

The shepherd's rod is a comfort in shadowy places. Literally, the shepherd's rod is a club, a club used to beat off the wolves which attack his flock. We cannot overcome the enemies in the shadows, but the shepherd defends us, even unto death. "I lay down my life for my sheep," Jesus said.

41

The shepherd's staff is a comfort for two reasons. First of all, it is used to keep us in the flock. As we start to stray, we feel the staff on our backside as a reminder that our life depends on staying together with the flock.

Second, the staff has a crook which can be used to rescue strays, even from dangerous ledges where they have fallen due to their foolish wanderings. You can picture the caring shepherd, leaving the 99 and seeking out the stray sheep. Finding the lost sheep on a ledge of a cliff, the shepherd leans down, gently puts the crook beneath its belly and lifts it back to safety.

"The Lord is our shepherd" — someone who cares enough to protect you when you are in need, and loving enough to find you when you are lost. The Lord is also the master of ceremonies at a banquet table at which I am a guest of honor. David was a shepherd and a king. Both themes show up in this psalm. But you are getting tired now. Let me tell you about the King who invites us to the great banquet tomorrow.

Day Three

As the pastor entered the room he noticed that the woman had a tray of food near her bed. He began his explanation of the twenty-third psalm by talking about food.

Food and fellowship are frequently used in the Bible in describing happiness, even heaven itself. How many times did Jesus say, "The kingdom of heaven is like a great banquet...?" To those who are low, who feel like nobodies, God announces good news in this psalm: you are kings and queens at the banquet table of the King of kings. Festivity in the midst of adversity is the theme of part two of this inspirational psalm.

The imagery changes in this psalm, from a shepherd's poem to a kingdom banquet. In the midst of our enemies, he prepares a banquet. The communion

42

of eating together, of celebrating together, even as enemies are round about us, should be a comfort to us. "Who would think of eating at a time like this?" someone might ask. "God's people," is the answer. They have someone else to defend them. With all kinds of problems, troubles and even enemies assailing us, we go to the banquet of our God to receive the body and blood (the life) of our Lord. We come in confidence and in faith because of the goodness and mercy of our God.

"Thou anointest my head with oil" means that we are sons and daughters of the king, a noble class. The ancient Hebrew custom of anointing the new king is the point of reference. We sometimes think of ourselves as nobodies. God sees the regal nature of his two-footed handiwork. The blessings God bestows upon his noble sons and daughters cannot be contained.

"What do you think of when I say, 'My cup overflows'?" the pastor asked. The patient didn't answer right away, so the pastor went on:

I see a picture of a little thimble beneath a waterfall. We are like thimbles. God's gifts come rushing into us and overflow beyond us. We cannot contain them. God's goodness and mercy are rich beyond description as we stop and think of the gifts which have been poured out upon us.

"Goodness" and "mercy" come from the Hebrew word *hesed* which means steadfast love and faithfulness in God. Whatever your orientation toward God may be — fickle or faithful — his orientation toward you is *hesed* — faithfulness.

"Surely goodness and mercy shall follow me all the days of my life." We had some friends whose little girl used to love to sing the song, "Surely Goodness and Mercy." It was always such a bright and cheerful experience to hear from a child the heart of the gospel message. She was singing about the fact that we can count on God because he keeps his promises.

"I think my granddaughter used to sing that song too," the patient said. "Good," said the chaplain. "Are you up to hearing more?" "Yes," she said.

Think back on your life — the narrow escapes, the near misses, the temptations to which you nearly succumbed. We are precariously situated "fiddlers on the roof" who are about to fall at any moment, as the play by that name says. As we look back on our lives, we realize how important the constant goodness and mercy of God are. Faith is what keeps us from falling and faith is a gift of God — a response to God's goodness and mercy toward us.

Dwelling "in the house of the Lord" originally meant going to the sanctuary to worship. Its larger meaning is caught in the promise of Jesus: "He who believes has eternal life."

God cares. We care because he cares. Like a shepherd, he leads us. We celebrate his care by caring. No wonder this is one of the most beloved passages of all. It speaks to us about the heart of God. Jesus said, "I am the Good Shepherd."

On the third day, as the pastor finished his explanation of the twenty-third psalm, the dying woman said, "Thank you. I had forgotten..." She closed her eyes. Two days later she died...in peace for the first time in 70 years.

Questions For
Reflection Or Discussion

1. Have you ever visited a dying person?

2. Describe his or her condition.

3. How did you feel about the visit?

4. How has Psalm 23 affected your life?

5

I Am The Door

*So again Jesus said to them, "Very truly, I tell you, I
am the gate for the sheep. All who came before me are
thieves and bandits; but the sheep did not listen to them.
I am the gate. Whoever enters by me will be saved, and
will come in and go out and find pasture. The thief comes
only to steal and kill and destroy. I came that they may
have life, and have it abundantly. I am the good shepherd. The good shepherd lays down his life for the sheep."*
— John 10:7-11 (NRSV)

Doors are interesting things. While mailing a package at the
post office recently a woman asked me to help her with her car
door because it wasn't working properly. "Do you know anything
about doors?" she asked. I almost told her, "Well, as a matter of
fact I've been working on a sermon on Jesus the door and I'd be
glad to tell you all about the nature of this spiritual door," but she
seemed interested in more practical matters, so I temporarily fixed
the latch in the car door and advised her to get to a garage and have
it repaired. As she drove away I thought, "Doors are very important to us, but we generally don't think about them unless something goes wrong with them."

Think about doors with me for a few minutes. They can be
used to keep people in or to keep them out. They can be used to
guarantee privacy, if they are closed, or to invite people in if they
are open. How many doors do you have in your house? Count
them. Maybe you have ten or 12, maybe more. Are they for keep-
ing people out or inviting them in?

Some doors are made of glass; some of metal. Most doors are made of wood. We focus here on wood doors. When doors are made of wood, then a tree had to lose its life in order for a door to be made. Jesus was a carpenter by trade and knew the story of the death of trees in order to produce wood for doors. Jesus gave up his life in order to become the door to life for others.

Jesus came to serve. He set his face toward Jerusalem toward the end of his life. It was there, on a tree, that he spent his last lonely hours as a servant and stricken slave in order to give people eternal life and set them free. He spoke eloquently about how service would carry him to death — even as his followers were arguing about greatness:

> ... *Whoever wishes to be great among you must be your servant, and whoever wishes to be first among you must be your slave; just as the Son of Man came not to be served but to serve, and to give his life a ransom for many.*
>
> — Matthew 20:26-28 (NRSV)

Jesus, like a tree, was killed in order to become the door to eternal life. When the Gospel of John uses the term "life" (John 10:10) or "eternal life" (John 3:36), it means a special quality of life on both this side of the grave and on the other side.

Jesus Is The Door To Abundant Life Here And Now

There are many voices promising happiness for the present. People buy books, go to lectures and spend millions of dollars trying to find the elusive bird of happiness. There are many false prophets who promise it. False prophets do not deliver it.

Jesus said, "I am the door." He didn't just point to the door. He said that he is the door to life. You can tell false religious teachers because they point to themselves or to their teaching as the door instead of pointing to Jesus as the door. Jesus is the only one who has made the ransom by giving up his own life that others may have life. All other doors, no matter how ornate or attractive, are entrances to the kingdom of death. Jesus, the door, leads to the kingdom of abundant life. What is life? How is it received?

John 3:36 points us to the answer to the first question. Abundant life is a quality of life which Jesus gives: "He who believes in the Son has eternal life." Note the present tense of the promise. Faith means having a living relationship with God now. The Gospel of John calls this relationship eternal life. Eternal life is not just something we go to when we die, but something we experience here and now through faith. The present experience of eternal life is imperfect because of sin, but the point is that eternal life is not just reserved for out yonder in heaven.

How do we receive this abundant life? It is accomplished by Jesus' death on the cross. It is appropriated by faith in Christ's suffering and death. We appropriate what Jesus has accomplished.

Jesus accomplished the task of giving us life in abundance. In Eastern countries in Jesus' time the shepherd literally laid his body in front of the flock as the door, providing safety from prowling and marauding dangers and giving a full life to those he loved — his sheep. Full life is what is offered here.

Seductive promises from the world are hollow. It is through Christ that we have love. It is through Christ that we have true peace. It is through Christ that we have eternal life.

Lively life is what Jesus has accomplished for those who come in and go out through him. Our part is to appropriate what has been accomplished.

Here, for instance, is a man — let's call him John — who has been in the church all his life, but has had only a ritualistic, rigid kind of faith. Frequently judgmental, he has maintained an official Christian "stance," but has none of the fruits of true faith — no true love for anyone but himself, no true peace or joy. His religion is a religion of true doctrines and moral behavior, but there is no joy, no abundant life. He is a humanist who calls himself a Christian. He is a good man but he has no relationship with Christ. One day, while in the hospital, he realizes the hypocrisy of his life and places his life in God's hands. Thus he learns to "come in and go out" through Christ and experiences for the first time in his life the fullness of his baptismal relationship with God. In baptism, God claimed him for one of his sheep, but not until later in life — through suffering — did John appropriate the power of his baptism to "come in and go out" through Christ, the door.

A man named Legion (Mark 5:1-20) approached Jesus one day and discovered that his inner, divided nature could be healed by this man who claimed to be the door to life. How many people are like Legion — divided, lonely, feeling no worth, striking out at people around them!

Jesus showed Legion and has since shown the legion brothers and sisters of the divided world how to find wholeness and life — through trust in him by "coming in and going out" through him.

A recovering alcoholic friend told me, "I get up every day and tell God that I am completely in his hands. I cannot stay sober without him. I must lean on and trust in Christ or I am lost." That's what it means to come in and go out through the door. We come into a world of faith in God through Christ the door, and thus when we are safe in the fold, or out in the dangerous world, we are under the watchful eye of the Lord.

Jesus said, "I came that they may have life and have it abundantly." I believe that he was talking about transformed lives this side of the grave and transformed lives on the other side of the grave.

Jesus Is The Door To Life After Death

A man once asked me, "Is Christianity a religion for the here and now or for after death?" "Yes," I replied. Christianity is not centered in one or the other. Jesus gives transformed life now and life with God after death. Jesus is not only the door to the more abundant living now, but also the door through which we go on the way to life after death.

I met a man on a plane one day who, when he found out I was a minister, shared his reservations about eternal life with me. "I've been a Presbyterian church member all my life," he said, "and I've even served on our church council, but I've never been able to believe that Jesus came back to life after death or that anyone else can." As we talked, it became increasingly obvious not only that he had doubts as many Christians do, but that he was judging Christian

50

doctrine by the yardstick of his own reason. The moral teachings of Jesus worked, so he believed in them. The spiritual elements of faith — especially life after death — troubled him because they could not be verified by reason.

I'm afraid that there are many church members of every denomination who have the same trouble. They want to use Christ to have a happier life here and now, but they exclude those parts of Christianity which do not fit into the scheme of things as judged by reason. Reason for them becomes the idolatrous altar before which they worship. That kind of faith is anything but trusting Christ as the door through which we go to God.

On the other hand I have known hundreds of radiant Christians who not only see the value of Christ for the here and now, but truly trust him and his words about the world to come. I have seen what a difference that trust makes when it comes to suffering and death.

At the funeral service for the Rev. Robert Parker, a former associate pastor of mine, I said, "He was a man who was a cheerleader for God and who trusted the promises of God including the ones about life after death." Bob Parker was a leader of cheer. Just recently someone told me, "Pastor Parker was the most Christlike person I have ever known. He had many limitations as we all do, but his love for people caused children and adults to gravitate to him. He knew and reflected the abundant, eternal life in the here and now and anticipated eternal life to come." In the face of the obstacles to life, Bob had a way of charging problems which sometimes brought good results. I said this at his funeral service.

Pastor Larry Warren, another pastor on our staff, was our cross bearer at that funeral service for Bob Parker. He led the procession at the beginning of the funeral and the recession at the end of the service, only at the end he went out the wrong door. When he got back to the sacristy, he wrote a note on the blackboard: "Before thou chargest, looketh where thou goest."

Many people try wrong doors to get to eternal life. They are the man-made ones. The only door which leads to eternal life is Jesus Christ. Jesus knows where he is going. Therefore he can show us the way.

Jesus gives us an advance look into where we are going after death so that we go the right way. He is the right door through which we proceed to the Father. Bob Parker wanted to live, indeed through his faith and the intercessory prayers of his friends he lived for two years beyond what his doctor had predicted, but he also knew that it was just a matter of time before he would walk through Christ the door to the kingdom of God beyond.

Think of yourself as only having a limited time to live. After all, that is true for all of us. Think of yourself as one who has a living relationship with God through Christ now, imperfect though you may be. Think of yourself hearing the Lord speak these words personally, "I will see you again, on the other side of the grave. I know the way. I will be with you."

Or, think of yourself in a church building that is on fire. You rush to one of the doors, only to find that it is locked. Over that locked door and on every other exit you see a flashing neon sign: "No Exit." Now picture yourself looking around for some way out and seeing the Lord standing in front of the altar beckoning you by name: "Come unto me...I know the way...I am the way...I am the door through which you find life."

When you walk through a door from now on, perhaps you will think of Jesus.

Questions For
Reflection Or Discussion

1. Have you ever cut down a tree? Did anything unusual happen?

2. How is Jesus like a tree?

3. How many doors do you have in your house?

4. How is Jesus like a door?

5. In what ways is your life abundant?

6. In what ways is it less than abundant?

7. If you knew you had only a limited time to live, how would you spend it?

6

I Am The Bread Of Life

I am the bread of life. — John 6:35 (NRSV)

For the tradition which I handed on to you came to me from the Lord himself: that the Lord Jesus, on the night of his arrest, took bread and, after giving thanks to God, broke it and said: "This is my body, which is for you; do this as a memorial of me." In the same way, he took the cup after supper, and said: "This cup is the new covenant sealed by my blood. Whenever you drink it, do this as a memorial of me." For every time you eat this bread and drink the cup, you proclaim the death of the Lord, until he comes.
— 1 Corinthians 11:23-26 (NEB)

There are five questions which will help us get into the text, or better yet, get this text into us.

Where Did You First Commune?

The first question is, "Where were you when you first communed?" For me it was at Christ Lutheran Church, at Parkside and Barry, on the Northwest side of Chicago. I was 18 years old, having gone through a conversion experience and having just completed private instruction with the Rev. Gabriel Tweet, pastor at Christ Lutheran Church. I remember the vivid feeling of not being worthy to receive Christ in this holy sacrament. I remember the vivid sense of overwhelming joy at being able to think of myself as a Christian. Where were you at your first communion?

Please spend a few minutes recalling your first communion. Then turn to a friend (if you are in a group) and share what you remember. If you are reading this book privately, meditate on that first communion. In what church did you first meet God in Holy Communion? How did you feel?

Where Was God When You First Communed?

Now that you have thought about where you were at your first communion, I have another question. The second question builds on the first one. Where was God at your first communion? That's right! God was present in the bread and wine. That's the point. Communion is more than just information or ideas. God is really present.

That's what Saint Paul has in mind when he repeats the words of Jesus about Holy Communion as the new covenant or the new promise (1 Corinthians 11:24-25). God is really in this bread and wine. He promised he would be. God keeps his promises. We need to personalize this promise. Without personalizing communion, it is just a ritual.

How Do We Personalize This Promise?

The third question is "How do we personalize Holy Communion?" After weeks of training and education, young people make their first communion and hear these words, "The body of Christ for you." The first communion of young people helps all of us to personalize the sacrament and think again of what it means to receive the body and blood of our Lord. As we remember where we were and where God was in our first communion, it is easier to personalize the sacrament.

On Maundy Thursday, the day when Christ instituted the Sacrament of Holy Communion with his disciples, he was personal in his words to the apostles. "My body...my blood...," he said. Remembering this holy day helps all of us to personalize the meaning of receiving the Lord's Supper and discipleship. We personalize the sacraments by focusing on the promise of Jesus.

It has been estimated that there are 30,000 promises in the Bible.[1] Here we focus on the one promise called "the new covenant in my blood." As we do so, we will ask two additional questions: "Why go to church?" and "Why go to Holy Communion?"

Why Go To Church?

A story told by theologian Pat Keifert, who grew up in western North Dakota, should prove helpful in trying to answer this fourth question. When he was six years old, Pat stood up on a table and proclaimed, "I'm going to be a pastor." Since then, Pat has had to face the question, "Why go to church?" as put to him by his Uncle Ralph.

Uncle Ralph was the most successful member of Pat's family. He was a plumber. He owned his own business. He worked hard six days a week (Monday through Saturday) and wanted to play hard on Sunday. Uncle Ralph liked to fish. That was his chief way to play. In western North Dakota there are many lakes and rivers where Uncle Ralph loved to fish. Uncle Ralph didn't go to church very often. Over the years Uncle Ralph frequently asked Pat a very important question. "Why go to church?"

Pat tried many answers which didn't satisfy his uncle.

1. "It is commanded." That's true enough. After all, God had a commandment: "Remember the sabbath day, to keep it holy." While it is true that this commandment means that we are to worship each sabbath, Uncle Ralph responded, "I can worship while I fish."

Uncle Ralph quickly added, "The sabbath is also a day of rest. I can't rest very well in church. I rest better at the lake fishing."

Young Patrick learned his Bible and catechism and soon challenged Uncle Ralph with another statement: "We can't have communion at the lake. Jesus commanded that we take Holy Communion. When he instituted the sacrament, he commanded , 'Do this.' That's why we call it Maundy (mandate or command) Thursday," the young teenager told his uncle, quoting the pastor who had said this in confirmation class.

"I can commune with God in my own way," Uncle Ralph replied. "I can commune with God in nature."

Young Pat tried another idea with his uncle.

2. "We need to worship in church for fellowship," he said. Uncle Ralph really got the better of him on that one, Pat confessed. "There's no better fellowship than with my fishing buddies," he said. Pat was also a fisherman. He knew the special fellowship which fishing buddies have. Pat knew that Christian fellowship was deeper than fellowship of fishermen, but couldn't explain it to his "de-churched" uncle.

A third reason came into play as Pat became a young man.

3. "How about the Bible?" he asked one day. "We go to church to learn more about the Bible."

"Yes," replied his uncle, "but we can study the Bible at the lake when we fish." Pat knew that his uncle did not study the Bible on his fishing trips, but he also knew that it was theoretically possible.

A fourth reason to go to church came to Pat one day.

4. We go because of the presence of God. "I think I've got the better of you on that one," said Uncle Ralph. "If you've ever been at a quiet lake in the Black Hills of North Dakota at sunset, you can feel the presence of the Creator in powerful ways." Pat had often fished in the Black Hills. He knew that the Creator's presence could be felt there in a special way. Pat felt stumped until he discovered what today he calls the best reason for going to church and receiving Holy Communion regularly.

Why Receive Holy Communion?

Jesus said about Holy Communion, "This is the new covenant." Covenant means promise. When Jesus makes a promise, you can count on it. "Jesus might meet you as redeeming love in another place, but he has said that he will do it in the bread and wine," Pat said. Jesus can meet you in other places, but you should not neglect the one place He said He would be.

For example, if I were God and I said that I would meet you at a certain place, at a certain time, you would be a fool not to be there. If I were God and I said that I would meet you at Coco's

Restaurant at 2 p.m. on Friday, you would be foolish not to be there. I might also meet you at city hall at 8 a.m. or at the police station at 9 a.m., but if I were God and I said that I'd meet you at Coco's Restaurant at 2 p.m., you would be foolish not to be there.

That's how it is in Holy Communion. God has promised to be there. We are foolish to think that we can meet him in his redeeming love anywhere else.

While God can meet us anywhere, we should not think that we can set the time and place. God does that. He has promised that for our redemption, He would be in the Word and the sacraments. Therefore, we should believe his promise.

In the Word preached and the sacraments of Baptism and Holy Communion, Jesus has said, "I'll be there to redeem you." These are the only places God has promised to be as the redeemer. In nature, at lakes and golf courses, we may discover the wonder of God's creation, but only in the Word of God preached and in the sacraments do we have God's promise that what Jesus did for us on the cross is delivered personally to us.

"In church, we are receiving Jesus," Pat said. "We aren't just considering ideas about God. We are receiving God." God has promised to be there as redeeming love. We can count on that promise. When it comes to other contacts, God can and does send messengers. When it comes to redeeming love, God comes Himself. "This is my body. This is my blood," He says. "This is not an idea about me, which I want you to consider. This is Me in, through and mysteriously under the bread and wine." How do I know this is true? Jesus said so. He promised. Uncle Ralph, Jesus keeps his promises.

Uncle Ralph, in the preaching of the Gospel, Jesus is present. How do I know? Jesus said so. You can depend on his promise. The preaching of the Gospel delivers Jesus, not just ideas about Jesus, but Jesus in person. Romans 10:14-17 says:

> *But how can they call to him for help, if they have not believed? And how can they believe, if they have not heard the message? And how can they hear, if the message is not proclaimed? And how can the message be proclaimed, if the messengers are not sent out? As*

the scripture says, "How wonderful is the coming of
messengers who bring good news!" But not all have
accepted the Good News. Isaiah himself said, "Lord,
who believed our message?" So then, faith comes from
hearing the message, and the message comes through
preaching Christ. — (TEV)

Uncle Ralph, in the waters of baptism we are receiving Jesus, not ideas about Jesus, but Himself. We are not just thinking about Jesus. We are actually receiving Jesus. How do I know? Jesus said so.

"All authority in heaven and on earth has been
given to me. Go therefore and make disciples of all
nations, baptizing them in the name of the Father and
of the Son and of the Holy Spirit...and lo, I am with you
always, to the close of the age."
— Matthew 28:18-20 (RSV)

There are lots of "Uncle Ralphs" out there, telling you that they believe in God in their own way, that they don't need church. They say that they know God in nature. To be sure, the Creator God is out there in beautiful sunsets, wide green golf courses and wonderful forests and lakes. But the God of redemption comes to us as promised — in Word and sacraments. Don't fall for the illusion that we can meet God where we want to, when we want to, on our own terms. The covenant has been established by God, not by us. The new covenant in Jesus' blood, the blood of the cross, is Holy Communion. That's the promise. God is there. We are called to be there, too. In Word and sacraments we meet God himself.

The Irish have a tradition about the word "Himself." It is reserved for someone of extreme importance. In Word and sacraments, we meet Himself.

Why receive Communion? Because it is commanded. Yes, but there is more. The promise of a presence of God is like none other. "I will save you, forgive you, and redeem you through Word and sacraments. I'll be there. You can count on it. I have promised

60

that it will be so. You can believe my promise," says the great I AM, Himself. *"I am the bread of life,"* he says (John 6:35).

Where were you at your first communion? Were you in Chicago, or Minneapolis, or Fountain Valley, California? Where was God at your first communion? He was there in the bread and wine. How do you know? He said so. He promised. You can depend on the promise. God is in this bread and wine. You can count on it. He promised. God never breaks a promise.

---

1. Herbert Lockyer, *All The Promises Of The Bible*, Zondervan, Grand Rapids, Michigan, 1984, p. 10.

Questions For
Reflection Or Discussion

1. Do you know anyone like Uncle Ralph? What is he like?

2. While no one will be argued into the kingdom of God, is it possible to explain the promise to someone like "Uncle Ralph"?

3. What is the difference between the God of creation and the God of redemption?

7

I Am The Real Vine

I am the real vine, and my Father is the gardener.
Every barren branch of mine he cuts away; and every
fruiting branch he cleans, to make it more fruitful still.
You have already been cleansed by the word that I spoke
to you. Dwell in me, as I in you. No branch can bear
fruit by itself, but only if it remains united with the vine;
no more can you bear fruit, unless you remain united
with me. I am the vine, and you are the branches. He
who dwells in me, as I dwell in him, bears much fruit;
for apart from me you can do nothing.
— John 15:1-5 (NEB)

In chapter four where we focused on the sheep staying together and staying under the guiding presence of the Good Shepherd. Here we focus on more than the guidance of God. We focus on abiding in Christ, staying close to and actually dwelling in Christ. Jesus says, "I am the vine, and you are the branches...apart from me, you can do nothing" (John 15:5 — NRSV).

This principle of closeness leading to productive fruit bearing raises three questions: (1) What shall we do? (2) How shall we do it? (3) Why should we do it?

What?

Precisely, what is commanded here? Precisely, what does Jesus want from us? Precisely, what does the Lord, the Great I AM, want us to do? Nothing and everything!

63

Dwelling, or abiding, as some translations put it, is a matter of doing nothing. Dwelling is a matter of achieving nothing and receiving everything. We don't have to accomplish anything. As Jesus said from the cross, "It is accomplished." If our salvation is accomplished by the action of Christ on the cross, why are we commanded to dwell? What is this dwelling or abiding in Christ?

Some years ago, my wife Joyce and I bought a new refrigerator. When we got the new refrigerator home, I noticed a tag on the back of it. The tag read: "Void if detached."

The guarantee was only good if the tag remained in place. In like manner, but at a much deeper level, we are void if we are detached from Christ. We are called to remain attached to him. Otherwise, what has been accomplished is lost. What has been accomplished is still valid, but we personally lose the benefits of it if we do not continue to dwell in Christ. We don't have to do anything to make it valid; *we have to do something to make it valid for us.* We have to stay attached or dwell in Christ.

Dwelling is everything. As a grape vine is invalidated by trying to live on its own, we are invalidated by living on our own. We shrivel up and die, like so many branches that have been cut off from the source of life.

Our part is to stay close to God like a little girl crossing a busy street with her father. "I'll get you across the street," the father says, "just don't let go of my finger." We had three daughters. When they were little, they would go anywhere with me, even across a busy highway, if I held their hand. If they let go, and tried to make it on their own, they would surely have died.

What is your part in salvation? Just holding on to the hand of the Father whose hand holds you. That's nothing, and it is everything.

How?

How do I hold on and avoid the certain death which comes if I try to go it alone? By faith. By faith we dwell in Christ who is the real vine. We dwell like branches. We draw all our strength from him.

Faith means appropriating what has been accomplished. Jesus died for all, but not everyone receives the benefits resulting from what he has accomplished. Many know the facts or the information about Christ, but have never appropriated what has been accomplished.

It's like a check written for one million dollars. God writes the check to you. It is yours. He has done all that needs to be done. He gives you the check, with no hidden agenda. It's a gift. But if you don't sign it and cash it, you don't get the benefits.

Millions have never even heard that the check has been written. Millions more may know that it has been written, but they know only the facts about what Jesus did. They don't know that the check has their name on it. Still millions more know that Jesus has done something wonderful and that is supposed to be for them, but they fail to turn the check over, endorse it and cash it. Why? Because they are fearful. Fearful? Fearful!

Fears about my worthiness may keep me from appropriating what has been accomplished. None are worthy, no not one, the Bible teaches. That's true, but I don't have to be worthy to sign the check.

Fears of trusting anyone may haunt the minds of those who refuse to appropriate what has been accomplished. With so many dysfunctional families where children have trusted parents, only to discover that the parents cannot be trusted; with so many cases of physical and emotional desertion; with so many cases of divorce where spouses fear being hurt again if they trust someone, fear keeps many out of the kingdom of God. "Believe, just trust me," God says.

Fears of expectations also keep some people as outsiders to real faith, really abiding. What will God expect of me? To be perfect? To become a missionary to Africa? To follow the rules? To stop my resentment? To shut down my fears? "I can't! I just can't do it!" God's expectations are that you trust him to do for you what you can't do for yourself.

"Believe me," God says, "This check is for you. It is free. Just sign it, cash it and abide in me."

Linda had experienced shame as a child. The shame came because her father was an alcoholic. She was fearful about bringing any playmates home because her father might be drunk. He might beat her mother as the little girl had seen him do before. She had gone to Sunday school as a little girl, but as she told her college roommate who took her to church once, "It had not taken."

Linda married a man who was an alcoholic, like so many children of alcoholics do. She felt unworthy. At least she knew how alcoholics act. After years of torturous self-doubt, she had finally divorced this alcoholic husband.

Her first experience of grace came when she married a Christian man who truly loved her. He led her to church and to the Lord. "I don't know how to believe," she said. "Just accept the fact that God has accepted you," he replied. It took several years, but today she is a believing Christian whose life centers on Christ as the most important person in her life. "You are second," she told her husband, "right behind Christ." He replied, "That's how it is supposed to be. I'm not supposed to be number one." She has learned to abide in Christ by faith. She is now the chairperson of the hospitality committee in her church. She reaches out for other hurting people and invites them into the faith family.

Why?

Why abide in Christ? Because nothing else works as a center but God. Make anything else the center of your life and it will be dysfunctional. Job? Yes! Money? Yes! Family? Yes! Husband or wife? Yes! Children? Yes!

Only God works as the center of our lives. That's how we were made.

Making God the center means abiding. As the song says, "Abide with me, fast falls the eventide...."

Time is running out. Abide. Night is drawing near. Abide. Death is coming. Abide. That's all true enough, but it isn't big enough.

A master artist was teaching his students how to paint. They were hesitant, lacking in confidence. One student brought his painting to the master for review. It was a good painting, but lacked something. "Amplius, amplius, amplius," said the master, "make it bigger."

Abiding in Christ saves us when death comes. Abiding in Christ keeps us from what the book of Revelation calls "the second death," the big death, separation from God. Why abide? To avoid the ultimate death, separation from God, hell. Yes, but abiding helps us with more than death. It helps us with life. Amplius: make the answer to "Why?" bigger.

"Abide with me," Jesus says. "Trust me like a branch trusts the vine for life."

> As the Father has loved me, so I have loved you. Dwell in my love. If you heed my commands, you will dwell in my love, as I have heeded my Father's commands and dwell in his love.
>
> — John 15:9-10 (NEB)

Why dwell in Christ? For overcoming death? Yes, but paint it bigger. For life? Yes, but paint it bigger. For mission.

Many people today have little sense of direction and meaning. The mission of Christ is to reach everyone with the good news that Jesus died for them and rose that they might have eternal life. Those who abide in Christ spread the message by word and deed. That gives them a purpose in life.

The student brought his painting back to the master a second time. Freed up by the master's urging him to make it bigger, the student let out all his creative energy on his painting. "Now, you've got it," said the master.

"Now, you've got it," says our master to the woman who was the daughter of an alcoholic father, who has finally come to faith. "Now you are dwelling in me to bear fruit. I am the real vine. You are the branches."

Questions For
Reflection Or Discussion

1. Do you know anyone like Linda in this chapter? Describe her verbally or write down a few of her characteristics.

2. How is someone like Linda reached for Christ?

3. Looking at your background and your spiritual gifts, what might your mission be?

8

I Am Who I Am

*...Though he was in the form of God, (he) did not
count equality with God a thing to be grasped, but emptied himself,... being born in the likeness of men.*
— Philippians 2:6-7 (RSV)

*Jesus said to them, "Very truly, I tell you, before
Abraham was, I am."*
— John 8:58 (NRSV)

The most crucial question that was ever asked about Jesus is
the one the people asked as he came riding triumphantly into Jerusalem that first Palm Sunday: *"Who is this?"* (Matthew 21:10).

It is a familiar question. It was discussed by the apostles and
answered by Peter at Caesarea Philippi: "You are Christ (i.e. the
Messiah), the Son of the living God." It was asked in astonishment
by the apostles when Jesus commanded the waters and winds to
obey him. "Who is this," they asked, "that even the winds and
waves obey him?" It was asked indignantly by Jesus' enemies, the
religious authorities, when they saw him heal a lame man who had
been lowered through a roof, especially because Jesus not only
healed him, but declared the man forgiven. "Who do you claim to
be? Only God can forgive sins," they said. It is the question that
was on everyone's mind when Jesus raised Lazarus from the dead.
And it is the question which stood behind the famous Temple debate between Jesus and the religious authorities as reported in John
8:58. In John 8:58 Jesus answers the question by applying the Old
Testament name for God to himself: "I AM."

There are many titles for Jesus which partially answer the question: Who is this? "The prophet," "the king of Jews," "the Messiah" (the anointed one), "the Son of God," "the Son of David," "the Son of Man," "the Lord," "the Servant," and "the I AM" (from John 8:58).

One way to get at the question, "Who is this?" and the meaning of Christ's answer, "I AM," is by looking at the classic statement of Saint Paul in Philippians 2:6-7, "Though in the form of God...he emptied himself," and Martin Luther's explanation of the second article of the Apostles' Creed in the *Small Catechism*: "I believe that Jesus Christ, true God, begotten from eternity and true man, born of the Virgin Mary, is my Lord." Let's begin with the humanity of Jesus.

Jesus Is True Man

Luther, following the Bible, says, "Jesus was true man, born of the Virgin Mary." That Jesus is true man means that I need never feel that I am alone in dealing with my problems or my suffering. As man, Jesus came in the form of a servant. That service means identification with our suffering.

In the incarnation, Jesus came from heaven to earth. He came all the way into our suffering. He went to the bowels of the earth. He descended to the depths of hell for the sake of his beloved brothers and sisters. He took our problems and our suffering on himself when he took on flesh and died on the cross. Jesus came as a servant. Does that make a difference in your life?

Have you ever felt lonely? Jesus knows what it feels like to be alone and abandoned. Have you ever been tempted beyond your endurance? Jesus was there with you. Have you ever been frightened? You were not alone with your fears, even though you may have felt alone. That Jesus is human means that he understands.

Have you ever suffered physical or mental pain almost to the breaking point? You probably felt separated from everyone. You probably felt that no one understood what you were going through. That Jesus is true man, the Servant, means that he is there with you. Anyone who has ever experienced life in the raw, in its hellishness, should greatly appreciate the servanthood of Christ.

The I AM meets us in the depths as a servant. He is bone of our bone, flesh of our flesh, blood of our blood, our brother.

The One who understands you is standing with you. Jesus is human. He felt pain. He really died. He is also divine.

Jesus Is True God

Jesus came as human servant. "He emptied himself," Saint Paul says (Philippians 2:7). He also came as divine King. That, too, is the theme of the Bible. The New English Bible (NEB) translation of Philippians 2:6 says: "the divine nature was his from the first."

The divinity of Christ causes some people serious problems. The Jehovah's Witnesses, Mormons, and New Age religionists, for example, teach that Jesus was not divine. They confuse a lot of Christian people by their arguments against the Trinity, the Church's doctrine that God is Father, Son, and Holy Spirit. Trinity does not mean three gods, but one God in three persons. At the heart of the doctrine of the Trinity is the assertion that Jesus is "true God, begotten of the Father from eternity..."[1]

Some people in the church tell me that they have never heard this teaching about Jesus' divinity before. They have understood that Jesus is the Son of God, but have not understood that Jesus is divine. It is quite a struggle for many people to realize that Jesus is divine, even though this is clearly taught in many passages of Scripture, including the text in Philippians 2, "Though he was in the form of God..." and the first chapter of the Gospel of Saint John, where we read that the Word, that is Jesus, became flesh. Jesus is God in human form.

Who is Jesus? Jesus himself forgives sin in the midst of the protests: "But only God can forgive sin. Who do you make yourself out to be?" Jesus says plainly: "The Father and I are One." The Gospel of John says that Jesus is God become flesh. Paul says about Jesus: "In him (Jesus) the whole fullness of deity dwells bodily" (Colossians 2:9 — NRSV), and "...Christ Jesus, who, though he was in the form of God, did not count equality with God a thing to be grasped, but emptied himself, taking the form of a servant, being born in the likeness of men" (Philippians 2:6-7 — RSV).

The last passage from Philippians is especially helpful in dealing with the question, "Who is this?" We will never intellectually grasp the fullness of the deity of Jesus, so Jesus took on servanthood, i.e.

he became human, but Jesus is also the Lord of the universe. More importantly, he is my Lord.

The thrust of this chapter is not to just get people to accept a new idea which is a true Christian doctrine. That is true enough, but not big enough. It is important that we have our ideas clear and that we know the truth with our minds, and it is important that we have the right teachings, but it is also significant that the doctrine of the divinity of Jesus is personal. Jesus' full lordship can only be real if we personally accept him as God incarnate.

Precisely this is at stake. The idea that Jesus is King and Lord is not life-changing until I make it personal. The idea that Jesus is King in my life requires obedience, not just acknowledgment.

Jesus Is My Lord

Precisely this was at stake the day that Jesus got into a serious conflict with the religious authorities when he used the term, "I AM," for himself. These authorities accused him of seeking self-glorification. Jesus contended that he sought no honor for himself. Jesus accused the religious leaders of hypocrisy. Jesus said that the father of the Jews, namely Abraham, rejoiced in his coming. He wondered why the Jews did not. They responded, "Abraham died a long time ago, so did the prophets. How then can you say they rejoice in your coming?" They were asking him if he thought he was greater than Abraham and the prophets. "Who do you think you are?" they said. Jesus answered that he had not honored himself, but only the Father had honored him, and that Abraham had rejoiced in his coming. The Jews replied, "You are not yet fifty, and yet have you seen Abraham?" Jesus said, "Before Abraham was, I AM."

Jesus used God's name, I AM, for himself. He used it because he believed and taught that he was divine. It was a shocking statement for many of the people. They picked up stones to throw at him, because they believed that he had committed heresy. He had claimed God's name. Either he was a raving, egocentric maniac who should be locked up behind bars, or he was what he claimed to be, namely divine.

Consider another story — this one about a man named Moses.

Moses went up to a mountain one day and there he was confronted by the living God. Moses entered into dialogue with the living God. God said to Moses, "Moses, go down to Egypt." Moses said to God, "I cannot go." God said to Moses, "Moses, I'll go with you." Moses said to God, "I cannot go." God said to Moses, "Moses, you be my spokesman." Again, Moses objected. He said, "I am not eloquent." God said, "Moses, I'll go with you." Moses said, "I know, but I am still afraid." On and on went the debate, until God finally promised that he would send Moses' brother, Aaron, to be a spokesman for him. Moses finally agreed, but before he went, Moses asked: "Who shall I tell the people sent me?" He was asking for the name of God. God gave him this name: "I AM Who I AM" (Exodus 3:14 — NRSV).

God was telling Moses that he is the one who has no beginning and no ending, the Alpha and the Omega, the A and the Z, the beginning and the end of all things. God is the One from Whom All Things Come, and the One to Whom All Things Go. Remember this name: "I AM Who I AM." It is the name that Jesus used for himself in the eighth chapter of the Gospel of Saint John. No wonder the Jews picked up stones to throw at him! By using I AM for himself, Jesus was claiming divinity. That divinity has personal implications for faith today.

Jesus is the Lord, the ruler of heaven and earth. He is our Lord, the Lord of his whole family on earth. But most significantly, he is my Lord. I cannot grasp the meaning of his lordship over the galaxies and I cannot fully appreciate the meaning of his lordship over his whole family until I, through faith, commit myself to him as my Lord. Here we experience the power of the personal in our faith. It is not enough to accept the doctrine of the humanity of Jesus and the divinity of Jesus. I can intellectually agree to ideas without entering into personal relationship with God. The heart of our religion is the personal confession, *"Jesus is my Lord."*

Mary was reading what she felt was a rather dull book one night. She put it by her night table and left it there. Several nights later, she attended a party and met a dashing, handsome, and gifted young man. Everyone was attracted to him and everyone listened to his words. She got an opportunity to speak to him alone later that night. "What do you do for a living?" she asked. "I am a writer," he replied. When she got home that night she glanced at the book by her table and saw the author's name was that of the man she had just met. She picked up the book and read through the night, unable to put down the book which only a few nights before she had considered dull. The difference was that now she knew the author. That's how it is with the Bible.

That is the thrust of this confession, *"Jesus is my Lord."* The personal element makes everything come alive. It changes the way we read God's book, the Bible. Jesus is the author who stands behind the human writers of the Bible. Acceptance of Christ through faith changes the way we think and live.

Jesus can come triumphantly as the Lord into our lives. It is necessary, however, for us to accept him as our Lord and Savior. If we see him only as a good man, or if we see him only as some kind of a special Son of God (like us only more so), we are limiting him considerably, and he cannot come into our lives triumphantly. Jesus is the Lord, the Great I Am. That's true enough, but not big enough. What is big enough? Jesus is "my Lord and my God," as Thomas said. Jesus is the One who can bring us back to God and enlarge our lives so that we can be the people that we were intended to be when we were born. He identifies with my suffering and my weakness by taking on the garb of a nobody, a servant. He also does for me what no mere man can do: he died for me on the cross.

Someone in the crowd that first Palm Sunday cried out: "Who is this?..."

The people in the crowd responded: "Blessed be he who comes... Hosanna in the highest."

In the person of Jesus, the Great I AM came to town. Jesus, the Lord, comes to your town and your home, too. That's true. Does it make a difference?

---

1. Martin Luther, the explanation of the second article of the Apostles' Creed, *The Small Catechism, Book of Concord*, Concordia Publishing House, St. Louis, Missouri, 1957, p. 161.

Questions For
Reflection Or Discussion

1. Have you ever met the author of a book you were reading?

2. Did it make a difference in how you read the book?

3. Do you remember memorizing Luther's explanation of the second article of the Apostles' Creed in confirmation?

4. What difference did it make then?

5. What difference does it make now?

9

I Am The Servant

...Here am I among you like a servant.
— Luke 22:27 (NEB)

The old Gospel hymn, "I Love To Tell The Story," is a helpful point of departure as we begin looking at Jesus, the Servant.

> *I love to tell the story*
> *Of unseen things above,*
> *Of Jesus and his glory,*
> *Of Jesus and his love.*
> *I love to tell the story,*
> *Because I know it's true;*
> *It satisfies my longings*
> *As nothing else would do.*
>
> *I love to tell the story:*
> *How pleasant to repeat.*
> *What seems, each time I tell it,*
> *More wonderfully sweet!*
> *I love to tell the story,*
> *For some have never heard*
> *The message of salvation*
> *From God's own holy Word.*
>
> *I love to tell the story,*
> *For those who know it best*
> *Seem hungering and thirsting*

To hear it like the rest.
And when, in scenes of glory,
I sing the new, new song,
I'll sing the old, old story
That I have loved so long.

Refrain:
I love to tell the story;
I'll sing this theme in glory
And tell the old, old story
Of Jesus and his love. (LBW, #390)

The old gospel hymn, "I Love to Tell the Story," reminds us that "some have never heard the message of salvation from God's own holy word." This song also states that, "Those who know it (the story) best seem hungering and thirsting to hear it like the rest." This story of Jesus, the servant, becomes dearer and nearer to us as we remember what happened and why it happened.

"Jesus, the Servant," is one of the themes in that old, old story. Jesus never said, "I am the servant," but there can be no mistake about the fact that that is what he meant when he said, "Here am I among you like a servant" (Luke 22:27).

In addition, in the enacted parable of the foot washing reported in John 13:1-17, the theme of servanthood is clear.

The Story Of The Foot Washing

When Mark, the host, did not wash the feet of his guests for the special Passover meals at his home, no one said anything. After all, it was a strange time and Jesus had said and done so many upsetting things, one couldn't blame Mark too much for forgetting the socially appropriate gesture of the host, washing his guests' dusty feet. The holy land is desert country. It left travelers with very dusty feet. Every Jewish host knew his obligation to start with a foot washing before serving a meal. The host saw himself as a humble servant of his guests for this purpose. But Mark was doing something else. He forgot his duty as a servant.

There was another Jewish tradition about foot washing, namely that the youngest member of a group was to do it. In other words, youngest was regarded as a servant for this purpose. The apostle John was the youngest member of the group. Like Mark, John neglected his duty to serve by washing the feet of the others. No one did the required foot washing.

What was everyone doing? Arguing about greatness.

Jesus observed that his followers were involved in an argument about who was to be the greatest in the kingdom of God. He got out the bowl and towel and went from one person to the other, washing their feet like a servant. It was an enacted parable. It is the story of Jesus, the servant, which has been told again and again, generation after generation. "Each time we hear it, it seems more wonderfully sweet," not sweet in a sentimental sense, but more dear to us and near to us. Each time we hear of the distance God came — from the highest heavens to the bowels of the earth — to save us, we can grow in our appreciation and love of the old, old story.

Jesus said, "...Here am I among you like one who serves" (Luke 22:27). The story of Jesus comes alive as we picture Jesus in selfless service. Servants think of taking care of the needs of others.

This story of Jesus, the Servant, becomes more dear to us and near to us as we consider the meaning of that servanthood as described by the prophet Isaiah:

> *He was despised and rejected by men; a man of sorrows, and acquainted with grief; and as one from whom men hide their faces he was despised, and we esteemed him not.*
>
> *Surely he has borne our griefs and carried our sorrows; yet we esteemed him stricken, smitten by God, and afflicted.*
>
> *But he was wounded for our transgressions, he was bruised for our iniquities; upon him was the chastisement that made us whole, and with his stripes we are healed.*

All we like sheep have gone astray; we have turned
every one to his own way; and the LORD has laid on
him the iniquity of us all.

He was oppressed, and he was afflicted, yet he
opened not his mouth; like a lamb that is led to the
slaughter, and like a sheep that before its shearers is
dumb, so he opened not his mouth.

— Isaiah 53:3-7 (RSV)

The cross of Christ is the fulfillment of the nightmarish proph-
ecy of Isaiah. The suffering servant, who washed the disciples'
feet, went even further on the cross. There he took the griefs and
sorrows of the world on his back. There he was stricken, afflicted,
wounded, bruised, and oppressed. There the Lord laid on him the
iniquity of us all. There he was slaughtered like a lamb, that the
blood of the lamb might be put on your doorpost and mine.

That brings us to the second part of the story of Jesus, the Servant: The Passover/Communion.

The Story Of The Passover/Communion

Jesus, the Servant, celebrated Passover with his followers after
the foot washing. After the custom of Moses, he passed the unleavened bread of Passover. This bread had been passed and con-
sumed in Jewish homes for 1,200 years to commemorate the freedom of the servant people Israel from Egypt. Unleavened bread
was used because the people were in a hurry to depart from Egyp-
tian slavery. They had no time to let bread rise.

This time, as Jesus raised the unleavened bread in the Passover
blessing, he said, "I have earnestly desired to eat this Passover
with you before I suffer; for I tell you, I shall never eat it again
until it is fulfilled in the kingdom of God... This is my body which
is given for you...This cup which is poured out for you is the new
covenant in my blood" (Luke 22:15-20).

Lamb's blood was placed on the wood doorposts of the Jews
that first Passover. It saved them when the angel of death passed
over their houses. Blood was also placed on the wood cross. It

was the blood of "the Lamb of God who takes away the sins of the world." That blood of life is given to us in the Sacrament.

Thus Holy Communion was instituted. Thus the blood of the Lamb of God, the sacrificial one, was put on your doorpost and mine. In Moses' day, the blood of the lamb was put on the doorposts of the Hebrews to identify the people of God so that the angel of death would pass over the homes of the chosen. Thus the old covenant was repeated and extended through Jesus on Maundy Thursday, Good Friday, and Easter. The blood of the new covenant is not the blood of a lamb, but the blood of the Lamb of God given in love.

I love to tell this story of Jesus and Jerusalem, of Moses and the Passover, of Maundy Thursday, Good Friday, and Easter. It seems each time I tell it, it is more wonderfully dear and near. It is a sad story of how far God will go to find you and me; and it is a glad story, for we can find new life in it. As we hear these words: "My body...my blood...for you...," we know that we are loved by the Great I AM, the Servant, who came and served even unto death, the death of the sacrificial Lamb of God.

Questions For
Reflection And Discussion

1. Has any family member made a sacrifice for you?

2. How did it make you feel?

3. How do hymns like, "I Love to Tell the Story," affect you?

10

I Am The Teacher

After he had washed their feet, had put on his robe,
and had returned to the table, he said to them, "Do you
know what I have done to you? You call me Teacher
and Lord—and you are right, for that is what I am. So
if I, your Lord and Teacher, have washed your feet, you
also ought to wash one another's feet. For I have set
you an example, that you also should do as I have done
to you. Very truly, I tell you, servants are not greater
than their master, nor are messengers greater than the
one who sent them. If you know these things, you are
blessed if you do them."

— John 13:12-17 (NRSV)

Jesus never said, "I am the teacher." Precisely, he said, "You call me Teacher and Lord — and you are right, for that is what I am." This chapter is an extension of the last one, "I Am The Servant." Here Jesus, the Great I AM is saying, "I expect you to be servants, too. Listen to what I say and do. Then follow what I have taught you. I am the teacher. You are my disciples." Guy Doud, 1986 National Teacher of the Year, said it well: "You can teach a wall, but when you help someone learn you have to get involved." Jesus got involved.

It is one thing to admire Jesus as a servant who gave up the power of being in the likeness of God to become a servant. It's another to follow him as a disciple. It's another to get involved.

83

Jesus, The Teacher

There are some people who admire Jesus as a teacher, but do not believe in him as Lord and Savior. They often say, "I like the morality of the Bible and I respect Jesus' words in the Sermon on the Mount, but I don't need a Savior; I don't want a Lord."

In the Bible where Jesus is called the Teacher, it doesn't just mean that he is a moral example. It means that the One who shaped heaven and earth descended to the depths, died for us on the cross, and showed us how to live. Without the cross of Christ, the teachings of Christ are just hollow humanism.

Humanism means trying to be good to our neighbors with no real reference to God. For the humanist, religion is a matter of doing good at the horizontal level, without the vertical dimension of trust in Christ. I know about humanism. I was a humanist for the first 18 years of my life.

My father was Jewish; my mother Irish Catholic. Since my father was opposed to the Roman Catholic Church, my mother stopped going. I had not attended church ten times before I started college at the University of Illinois in 1954. I was a good, moral person, but not a Christian before I was 18.

While studying to be an engineer at the University of Illinois in Champaign-Urbana, I picked up three books on topics which I thought would help me avoid the label of "a narrow-minded engineer": *How To Know And Tell The Weather; The Universe And Dr. Einstein;* and *The Greatest Story Ever Told.* I did not think that I wanted to become a Christian. I just wanted to know more about the teachings of Jesus.

I read the book on Albert Einstein first. Albert set me up to meet God by saying that everything is relative. "If everything is relative," I thought, "then why try to be rich and successful?" Then I read the book on Jesus. I never got to the book on the weather. I still have it on my book shelf. I hope to read it some day when I retire.

In *The Greatest Story Ever Told,* I met Jesus, the Teacher, but it was not the morality of Jesus which fascinated me. It was the Teacher himself and what he did. I began reading the Bible and

84

found myself in almost every section except "the begats." The rest, as they say, is history. I left the University of Illinois and enrolled at Carthage College, Carthage, Illinois, to prepare for becoming a pastor. I discovered a new way of life through the Teacher. I got involved.

Jesus said, "You call me Teacher and so I am." We need to look at the teachings and the Teacher. The Teacher calls us across time and eternity to submit our stubborn willfulness and self-centeredness to him and follow him, not just his teachings. Like many humanists, I had been picking and choosing between the various ideas of the Bible which I tried to follow. I was trying to be good without God. Being good without God is not really possible. It's a way of life by which we try to stay in charge without letting God be God.

If we ignore the prime teaching of the Teacher, we do so to our destruction. The prime teaching of Jesus is that he is Savior and Lord.

Jesus, The Savior

That Jesus is Savior means that I need to be saved. Saved from what? From sin and from myself!

Sin is spelled S—I—N. The center of sin is "I." I had wanted to stay in the center and make my own decisions and go my own way. What I had to learn from the Teacher is that this way doesn't work.

No act of the self can lift the self out of the self by the self because the biggest problem I have is the self. That Jesus is Savior means that I have to submit myself to him daily and let him do what I can't do — save me from certain destruction.

For a moment think of yourself in a burning building, six stories up. You run to the window. Smoke and fire. You run to the staircase. Smoke and fire. You don't know what to do. Remembering the moral teachings of Jesus won't help. You run back to the window, looking for some sign of hope. You can't see anyone because of the smoke, but you hear a still, small voice: "Jump, I'll catch you."

You either jump or die. I jumped. It's called the leap of faith. I discovered that God was there to catch me. That's what it means to have a Savior.

Think of yourself as having fallen to a shelf on a mountain top, clinging to a branch on the side of the mountain. You cry out, "Is there anyone up there?" "Yes," comes a booming voice from above. "I am here." "What should I do?" "Let go." After some hesitation, you may be tempted to cry out like many do, "Is there anyone else up there?"

To find Jesus as Savior means to let go and let God do what only God can do, save us.

Jesus is the Teacher. He is the Savior. He is also the Lord.

Jesus, My Lord

That Jesus is Lord means that he reigns. That Jesus is my Lord means that he reigns in my life. How different this is from merely being moral and trying to follow the teachings of Jesus.

The lordship of Christ means that the kingdom of God is my home. The kingdoms of this world are all temporary residences which do not satisfy our longing for home. Our tendency to try to have it "my way" is the very sin described in the first chapter of the Bible. Right from the beginning we see that, like Adam and Eve, we want to live life "my way." To submit to the lordship of Christ changes everything.

Gert Behanna was married and divorced three times. She was a millionaire. She had everything that people say they want. In her own words, she said that she had nothing. When she became a Christian and submitted to Christ's leadership of her life, she had everything.

Gert was an alcoholic. She had passed over that fine line of being a social drinker to being addicted to alcohol. After she tried suicide and failed at taking her life, a Christian friend wrote that she should come for a visit. She got drunk to meet her first Christians. "That's more of a commentary on us Christians than on us drunks," she said later. "So, you believe in Jesus, do you?" she said. "So, he helps you with your problems, does he?" she taunted. "Why don't you just turn your life over to him?" her friends said.

"Like I turn my luggage over to a porter?" she asked. "Yes," they said, "something like that." "These friends let me have our Lord as a porter," she said later. "They did not correct my theology. They let me start where I was." When she got home from her visit with her first Christians, she opened her mail and to her surprise she found a note from her friends and an article by Sam Shoemaker called, "It's Never Too Late To Begin Again." She read it and dropped to her knees. She started to pray the only prayer she had ever heard. "Our Father..." she said.

Then she stopped. "If I have a heavenly Father," she thought, "then all the people of the world are my brothers and sisters."

That's what it is like when Jesus becomes Teacher, Savior and Lord. We want to treat other people the way he did, as family. That's why we serve others. That's the way Jesus did it. He got involved. So do we.

Questions For
Reflection Or Discussion

1. Were you raised as a Christian?

2. What do your humanist friends say about God? Jesus? Church?

3. From what does Jesus need to save us?

4. Do you have any alcoholics in your family or among your friends?

5. If so, what have they learned about God?

6. What can we learn from them?

11

I Am Making All Things New

(Including You)

...He who sat upon the throne said, "Behold! I am making all things new!"

— Revelation 21:5 (NEB)

"Father, forgive them, for they know not what they do."

— Luke 23:34 (RSV)

Revelation 21:5 hardly seems like an appropriate text to mix with the Good Friday words of Jesus about forgiving those who are crucifying him. The Good Friday verse focuses on the death of Christ. Revelation 21:5 focuses on the ultimate reign of Christ. Good Friday is gory. Revelation 21:5 is about glory.

Yes, but in a sense, the cross of Christ is his throne. Jesus, the king of the universe, rules as the Suffering Servant. Good Friday is a time to think about our sins which put Jesus on the cross, but the cross also tells us that Jesus conquers our sins, and makes "all things new." Victims become victors as we behold the man on the cross, the one who suffered and died that we might have life eternal. Jesus is the one who makes all things new. Jesus' cross is the way by which God accomplishes this task.

These words, "I am making all things new," have a strange but wonderful connection to the crucified One. It is as if in each word from the cross, Jesus is telling us: "This is the way I am making all things new." Jesus starts with forgiving his enemies and ends with,

"It is accomplished." He is declaring in the first and the last words of the cross that the victory is won. This is not just a victory for all people. It is a victory for you.

If this formula from the last book of the Bible, "I am making all things new," is enlarged by the words, "including you," it takes on a personal meaning as we connect it to Jesus' words from the cross. Bear with me for a few minutes and see if the ancient, old words of our Lord from the cross don't take on a special meaning for you when you connect them to your life through this formula: "I am making all things new... including you."

Jesus' Words From The Cross

Jesus' first word from the cross was, "Father, forgive them, for they know not what they do" (Luke 23:34).

The words apply to the Roman soldiers who crucified Christ. As they walked from the place of the trial to Golgotha, "the place of the skull," perhaps they thought:

> *We are crucifying a criminal. It was a dirty job, but capital punishment is necessary. You can't let people who break the Roman law get off free. They must be punished. What would the world be like if we didn't properly punish wrongdoers? Jesus is guilty or the government would not have turned him over to us to crucify. It's a dirty job, but someone has to do it. Step lively, Jesus. Let's get on with it.*

They didn't know what they were doing. Neither did the Roman governor.

Pontius Pilate tried to set Jesus free. "Do you want Barabbas or Jesus?" he pleaded with the crowd. Pilate had a scheme which would allow him to set the obviously innocent man Jesus free. The crowd surprised him. "We want Barabbas," they cried. What could he do? He had to "save face." Pilate didn't know what he was doing. Neither did the crowd. They just got trapped by the Jewish high priests and their co-workers of evil. The crowd didn't know what they were doing because they didn't know that Jesus was making all things new by the cross.

The Jewish high priests, Caiaphas and Annas, didn't know what they were doing either. They thought that they were just doing their job protecting the people from a potentially dangerous man who claimed to be the Messiah. Of course, their jealousy and fear were part of the mixture of intrigue and deceit. Yes, they held court in the middle of the night, a thoroughly illegal procedure for the Jewish court, the Sanhedrin, but what do you do with a man like this? If they had held court at the legal times, someone might have shown up and witnessed to Jesus' innocence. You understand, don't you? They had to do it this way, away from the crowds of people Jesus helped. The crowds might riot. They didn't know what they were doing. They did not know what Jesus was doing.

Neither did the apostles. In stops and starts and varying degrees they had been loyal and faithful for three years. They had seen the tenderness and the power of Jesus. They didn't expect it to end like this. It must not end like this! They scattered like scared sheep when Jesus was arrested. They didn't know what they were doing.

If Peter knew what he was doing, do you think he would have declared that he didn't even know the man? He did that three times. If Peter knew that his denials would be reported millions of times every year, year in and year out, would he have ever said, "I don't know him"? When the cock crowed, Peter remembered that Jesus had said that it would happen just like this. But Peter, we understand that you didn't know what you were doing when you betrayed your best friend, the best friend a man could ever have. Peter did not know what he was doing. Neither did Judas.

Judas thought Jesus was a powerful ruler who would overthrow the Romans and lead the Jewish Zealots to victory over their oppressors. Surely, Judas did not expect it would turn out like this. They arrested Jesus. They tried him like a criminal. They prepared him for crucifixion. Judas didn't know what he was doing. Pitiful Judas committed suicide before the words from the cross were spoken, "Father, forgive them for they don't know what they are doing."

Judas, if you had only known, if you had only waited, if only you had heard the first words from the cross about forgiveness...if only you had hung on instead of hanging yourself. If only...but you didn't know what you were doing. Neither do we.

As we look at all these people around the cross, we ask, "Jesus, what are you doing up there?"

We Don't Know What We Are Doing

Worst of all, we don't know what we are doing. By our sin, we nail Jesus to the cross. "Jesus, what are you doing up there, stripped and dying like a common criminal? Jesus, why did the Jewish authorities and the Roman authorities do this to you?" we plead.

Listen closely to the answer:

"Not them. You. Every time you sin, every time you lust or lie, every time you worship and follow false gods or use my name in vain, every time you dishonor someone, or hate someone, or use someone, or covet someone else's possessions ... you crucify me. Not them. You."

We don't know what we are doing.

Jesus, what are you doing up there on the cross?

"Making all things new, including you..."

"Including me?"

"Even you!"

"By my death, I am making all things new. I am giving all things a new beginning. I am making new life possible for every man, woman, and child, every living creature.

"I am paying the price for sin. I am forgiving all who have offended. I am saying that the new age, the age of forgiveness, has begun. I am making all things new, even you."

"Yes, I understand you are dying for all people everywhere."

"No, you do not understand until you know that all of this suffering, all of this agony, is for you as if there were not another person on the face of the earth. I am making all things new, including you."

But if that is true, then I crucified you. My sins put you there...not the Romans, not the Jewish authorities, but my sins put you there.

"Yes, son. Yes, daughter. Now you understand. All of this is for you, as if there were only you. That's how much I love you. That's how much I care. I make all things new, even you."

"Is that what you are doing up there? I didn't know what I was doing."

"Yes, I know. That's what I am doing up here. I am making all things new."

"Even me?"

"Especially you!"

Questions For
Reflection Or Discussion

1. What is your first recollection of Jesus from childhood?

2. Have you ever seen anybody die? Under what conditions?

3. Who killed Christ on the cross?

12

I Am The Resurrection
And The Life

Jesus said to her (Martha), "I am the resurrection and the life. Whoever believes in me will live, even though he dies..."

— John 11:25 (TEV)

Tony Campolo tells the story of a black Baptist preacher in the inner city of Philadelphia who preached a sermon Tony says he'll never forget. Tony preached first. He was "hot," so "hot" he says, that he even stopped and listened to himself. He sat down and said to his pastor: "Now see if you can top that one!"

"Son," said the black pastor, "you ain't seen nothin' yet." For an hour and a half the pastor repeated these words over and over again: "It's Friday, but Sunday's a comin'."

"I've never heard anything like it," Tony said. "He just kept saying it. The congregation was spellbound by the power of it."

> *"It's Friday. Mary, Jesus' mother is crying her eyes out. That's her son up there on the cross. He's dying the agonizing death of crucifixion as a criminal. But it's only Friday," the preacher said. "Sunday's a comin'.*
>
> *"The apostles were really down and out. Jesus, their leader, was being killed by evil men. But it was only Friday. Sunday is a comin'.*

> *"The Devil thought he had won. 'You thought you could outwit me,' he said, 'but I've got you now.' But it was only Friday. Sunday is a comin'."*

"He went on like that for 30 minutes, 40 minutes, an hour. Each time he said, 'It's Friday,' the crowd began to respond, 'but Sunday's comin'. An hour and 15 minutes.

> *"It's Friday and evil has triumphed over good. Jesus is dying up there on the cross. The world is turned upside down. This shouldn't happen. But it's only Friday. Sunday's a comin'.*
>
> *"It's Friday. But Sunday is comin'. Mary Magdalene was out of her mind with grief. Her Lord was being killed. Jesus had turned her life from sin to grace. Now he was dead. But it's only Friday. Sunday is a comin'."*
>
> *The place was rocking. For an hour and a half.*
> *"Friday! But Sunday is a comin'. Friday. But Sunday is a comin'.*
>
> *"The sisters and the brothers are suffering. It just isn't fair...all they have to go through, but it's only Friday. Sunday is comin'."*

"I was exhausted," Tony said. It was the best sermon I've ever heard. The old preacher was saying it and the people were with him. "It's Friday, but Sunday is a comin'." "It was powerful," Tony said. "It was personal."

That's the Easter message! Sunday is comin'! Jesus is the Great I AM getting crucified, and yet changing the world as the resurrected one.

The Power Of The Personal Call Of God

One of the most poignant scenes in human history came in the early morning darkness of that first Easter when Mary Magdalene arrived at the tomb of Jesus planning to anoint his dead body, only to discover that the tomb was empty. Sure that someone had stolen the body of Jesus, Mary ran to tell the other disciples. Peter and John ran ahead and found the tomb as Mary had said. By the time Mary got back she was exhausted and weary with grief and worry. She stood weeping outside the tomb, her eyes red and swollen, her heart broken. When she looked into the tomb, she saw two angelic beings who asked her, "Woman, why are you weeping?" She said to them, "Because they have taken away my Lord, and I do not know where they have laid him." Then turning, she saw a man in the gray morning light whom she supposed to be the gardener. "Sir, if you have carried him away, tell me where you have laid him, and I will take him away." Gently, the risen Jesus said, "Mary." He had spoken her name many times before.

Jesus took the initiative. The first thing that happened when Jesus came back from the grave was that he said her name, "Mary." God always takes the initiative. Jesus said, "Mary," before Mary said, "Rabonni." Put your name in that story that the power of God's personal initiative may come through.

It is not only the discovery of the resurrected Lord which moves us in the story, but the element of the personal — the use of names. Mary had found the meaning of her life when she first met and followed Jesus. Jesus had given her a feeling of dignity and worth. When he had called her by name, it had always moved her deeply because each new encounter with him was an adventure in personal growth. Now, in the dawn of that first Easter morning, Mary Magdalene heard the first word spoken by the risen Lord: "Mary" — her name.

The one who calls us is the Great I AM. "I am the resurrection and the life," Jesus said (John 11:25) at the tomb of his friend, Lazarus. Lazarus discovered the powerful, personal call of the Resurrected One.

Jesus' friend Lazarus, of Bethany, had died when Jesus was away. When Martha saw Jesus, she said, "If only you had been here, Lazarus would not have died." She seemed near despair. Jesus said, "He will rise again." When she responded, "Yes, I know that he will rise again at the last day," the Lord said, "I am the resurrection and the life."

It is not surprising that we are loved by our peers or friends. It is amazing that we are known and loved by someone who is the Lord of the heavens and the earth — The Lord of Life, the Great I AM.

Jesus knew and loved Lazarus. Jesus faced the tomb and called out, "Lazarus, come forth." And he did! That's the power of a personal call from God. "Lazarus," Jesus said. That's personal power which keeps us from despair. Put your name there and hear the call of God. "John ... Mary ... Harry ... Ron ... Joyce ... Diane ... come forth."

Jesus said, "I am the resurrection and the life." That means power, personal power over death itself for you and me. I have heard many people say: "God is too busy with important matters to bother himself with me and my little problems." The biblical corrective for the feeling of worthlessness and the fear of despair is this simple and personal word from the resurrected Lord, "Lazarus." Put your name there. God is speaking your name. "Mary...Joe...Betty, 'Come forth.'" Jesus calls us back from the dead, too. It isn't just a call to the physically dead, but to the spiritually dead, too.

Many are physically alive, but spiritually dead. Jesus is calling them just as surely as he called Lazarus. "Come forth," Jesus says. "I am the resurrection and the life...I died for you. Do you hear me? I died for you."

A mother living in a tenement house went shopping for groceries. While she was in the store, a fire engine raced by. She wondered, "Is the fire engine going to my home?" She had left her baby asleep at home. Forgetting about the groceries, she ran toward home. Her building had fire hoses aimed at it. It was burning like a matchbox. Rushing to the chief, she cried out, "My baby is up there." He shouted back to her, "It would be suicide for anyone to go up there now; it's too late."

A young fireman standing by volunteered, "Chief, I have a little baby at home, and if my house were on fire, I'd want someone to go up to save my baby. I'll go." The young fireman climbed the stairs; he got the baby, threw her into the rescue net, and just as he did, the house collapsed and he was burned to death.

The scene is 20 years later at a graveside. A 20-year-old woman is sobbing softly. Before her, at the head of this grave, is the statue of a fireman. A man stopping by asks respectfully, "Was that your father?" She replies, "No." "Was that your brother?" "No," she says. "That's the man who died for me."

At a much deeper level, we can say that about Jesus: "That's the man who died for me. He died that I might live. He is the resurrection and the life."

God calls. We hear our names. We respond. We can appropriate what has been accomplished on the cross. We can make it ours. "Come forth," says the Great I AM. "Rabonni, my Lord and teacher," we can respond. Then we witness to others about the one who is the resurrection and the life. The 20-year-old woman said, "That's the man who died for me."

The Power Of The Personal Witness

A young father hadn't been home much nor had he been going to church with the family because of his strong drive for success. He was too busy to pay much attention to the family or God. His wife had witnessed for Jesus Christ, but seemingly to no avail. She had insisted that he put the child to bed that night. "Later," he said. "She hasn't seen you for weeks," his wife replied. Reluctantly, he went upstairs. "Let's sing, Daddy," the little girl said. Together they sang,

> *Praise him, praise him*
> *All ye little children*
> *God is love, God is love.*

> *Love him, love him*
> *All ye little children*
> *God is love, God is love.*

"Time for sleep," he said. "But, Daddy," the little girl had said, "you forgot to crown him." Together they sang,

> *Crown him, crown him*
> *All ye little children.*
> *God is love. God is love.*

As the father left the bedroom, he had a moving, life-changing thought:

> *"Maybe I haven't crowned him. I've let other things become too important. I've got to get back to God and church. My land, next Sunday is Easter. I haven't been to church in months."*
>
> *When he got downstairs, he announced to his wife. "We are going to church Sunday. It's Easter! I've been away from God too long."*

The wife's personal witness combined with his daughter's finally reached the father's hard head. The little girl knew the powerful, personal love of Jesus. Through her witness, the father heard Jesus call his name. He began the long journey back to the risen Lord. Through his daughter, he woke up to God's personal call to be a disciple of the Lord Jesus Christ.

Jeremy was born with a twisted body and a slow mind. At the age of 12 he was still in second grade, seemingly unable to learn. His teacher, Doris Miller, often became exasperated with him. He would squirm in his seat, drool and make grunting noises.

At other times, Jeremy spoke clearly and distinctly, as if a spot of light had penetrated the darkness of his brain. Most of the time, however, Jeremy irritated his teacher. One day Miss Miller called Jeremy's parents and asked them to come to St. Theresa's school for a consultation.

As the Forresters sat quietly in the empty classroom, Doris said to them, "Jeremy really belongs in a special school. It isn't fair to him to be with younger children who don't have learning problems. There is a five-year gap between his age and that of the other students."

Mrs. Forrester cried softly into a tissue, while her husband spoke. "Miss Miller," he said, "There is no school of that kind nearby. It would be a terrible shock for Jeremy if we had to take him out of this school. We know he really likes it here."

Doris sat for a long time after they left, staring at the snow outside the window. Its coldness seemed to seep into her soul. She wanted to sympathize with the Forresters. After all, their only child had a terminal illness. But it wasn't fair to keep him in her class. She had 18 other youngsters to teach, and Jeremy was a distraction. Furthermore, he would never learn to read and write. Why waste any more time trying?

As she pondered the situation, she prayed. "Oh God," she said aloud, "here I am complaining when my problems are nothing compared to that poor family! Please help me to be more patient with Jeremy!"

From that day on, Doris tried hard to ignore Jeremy's noises and his blank stares. Then one day, he limped to her desk, dragging his bad leg behind him.

"I love you, Miss Miller," he exclaimed, loud enough for the whole class to hear. The other students snickered and Doris' face turned red. She stammered, "Wh—why that's very nice, Jeremy. N—now, please take your seat."

Spring came and the children talked excitedly about the coming of Easter. Doris told them the story of Jesus, and then to emphasize the idea of new life springing forth, she gave each of the children a large plastic egg. "Now," she said to them, "I want you to take this home and bring it back tomorrow with something inside that shows new life. Do you understand?"

"Yes, Miss Miller!" the children responded enthusiastically — all except for Jeremy. He just listened intently; his eyes never left her face. He did not even make his usual noises.

Had he understood what she had said about Jesus' death and resurrection? Did he understand the assignment? Perhaps she should call his parents and explain the project to them.

That evening Doris' sink stopped up. She called the landlord and waited an hour for him to come by and unclog it. After that, she still had to shop for groceries, iron a blouse, and prepare a vocabulary test for that next day. She completely forgot about phoning Jeremy's parents. The next morning 19 children came to school, laughing and talking as they placed their eggs in the large wicker basket on Miss Miller's desk. After they completed their math lessons, it was time to open the eggs.

In the first egg, Doris found a flower. "Oh yes, a flower is certainly a sign of new life," she said. "When plants peek through the ground we know that spring is here." A small girl in the first row waved her arm. "That's my egg, Miss Miller," she called out.

The next egg contained a plastic butterfly which looked real. Doris held it up. "We all know that a caterpillar changes and grows into a beautiful butterfly. Yes, that is new life too." Little Judy smiled proudly and said, "Miss Miller, that one is mine!"

Next, Doris found a rock with moss on it. She explained that moss, too, showed life. Billy spoke up from the back of the classroom, "My Daddy helped me!" he beamed.

Then Doris opened the fourth egg. She gasped. The egg was empty! Surely it must be Jeremy's, she thought, and of course, he did not understand her instructions. If only she had not forgotten to phone his parents! Because she did not want to embarrass him, she quietly set the egg aside and reached for another.

Suddenly Jeremy spoke up. "Miss Miller, aren't you going to talk about my egg?"

Flustered, Doris replied, "But Jeremy — your egg is empty!" He looked into her eyes and said softly, "Yes, but Jesus' tomb was empty, too!"

Time stopped. When she could speak again, Doris asked him, "Do you know why the tomb was empty?"

"Oh, yes!" Jeremy said, "Jesus was killed and put in there. Then his Father raised him up!"

The recess bell rang. While the children excitedly ran out to the school yard, Doris cried. The cold inside her melted completely away.

Three months later Jeremy died. Those who paid their respects at the mortuary were surprised to see 19 eggs on top of his casket, all of them empty. Jeremy brought a powerful, personal witness to the one who said, "I AM the resurrection and the life."[1]

We all have Fridays where it seems like nothing is working. Suffering with its many problems, defeats, and failures seems to have an unbreakable hold on us.

But it is only Friday. The Great I AM is working resurrection and new life in our lives. "Sunday is comin'."

---

1. A story by Ida Mae Kemple.

Questions For
Reflection And Discussion

1. Do you remember any Easters from when you were a child? What was special about them?

2. Can you describe any gloomy "Fridays" when it seemed that nothing was working out right?

3. Have you seen any "Easter" reversals in your life?

4. Have you had some friend or relative die? How did the Great I AM make an appearance?

5. Who are some of the witnesses who have witnessed to God's resurrection story in your life?

13

I Am The Alpha And The Omega

*"I am the Alpha and the Omega," says the Lord
God, who is and who was and who is to come, the Almighty.*

— Revelation 1:8 (NRSV)

*It was late that Sunday evening, and the disciples
were gathered together behind locked doors, because
they were afraid of the Jewish authorities. Then Jesus
came and stood among them. "Peace be with you," he
said. After saying this, he showed them his hands and
his side. The disciples were filled with joy at seeing the
Lord. Jesus said to them again, "Peace be with you.
As the Father sent me, so I send you." Then he breathed
on them and said, "Receive the Holy Spirit. If you forgive people's sins, they are forgiven; if you do not forgive them, they are not forgiven."*

*One of the twelve disciples, Thomas (called the
Twin), was not with them when Jesus came. So the other
disciples told him, "We have seen the Lord!"*

*Thomas said to them, "Unless I see the scars of the
nails in his hands and put my finger on those scars and
my hand in his side, I will not believe."*

*A week later the disciples were together again in-
doors, and Thomas was with them. The doors were
locked, but Jesus came and stood among them and said,
"Peace be with you." Then he said to Thomas, "Put
your fingers here, and look at my hands; then reach out
your hand and put it in my side. Stop your doubting,
and believe!"*

Thomas answered him, "My Lord and my God!"

Jesus said to him, "Do you believe because you see me? How happy are those who believe without seeing me!"

In his disciples' presence Jesus performed many other miracles which are not written down in this book. But these have been written in order that you may believe that Jesus is the Messiah, the Son of God, and that through your faith in him you may have life.

— John 20:19-31 (TEV)

A popular monk in the Middle Ages announced that in the cathedral that evening he would preach a sermon on the love of God. The people gathered and stood in silence waiting for the service while the sunlight streamed through the beautiful windows. When the last bit of color had faded from the windows, the old monk went to the candelabrum, took a lighted candle and walked to the life-size statue on the cross. He held the light beneath the wounds on Jesus' feet, then his hands, then his side. Then, still without a word, he let the light shine on the thorn-crowned brow. "Amen," he said. That was his sermon. The people stood in silence and wept, knowing that they were at the center of a mystery beyond their knowing, that they were indeed looking at the love of God — a love so deep, so wide, so eternal that no words could express it and no mind could measure it.

Adoration of the Almighty is the heart of Christian worship. We know Almighty God as we fall at the feet of Jesus with Thomas and confess: "My Lord and My God." The Almighty on the cross is a mind-stirring paradox. Three Greek words are used in Revelation to lead us to adoration of the Almighty — alpha, omega, and pantokrator.

The Alpha And The Omega

This claim of God appears three times in the book of Revelation: 1:8, 21:6, and 22:13. In Revelation 22:13 we have Jesus'

106

parting speech to John on the island of Patmos. It is a vision of things as they really are and as they shall be. In that vision, Jesus says: "I am the Alpha and the Omega." That vision contains the revelation of the Alpha and Omega, the first letter of the Greek alphabet, and the last. Jesus is the first and the last — the ultimate, the "Totaliter Aliter" (a German theological term meaning "the totally other One"). Is there a way to make this confession more concrete? Thomas, the doubting apostle, shows us one way.

Thomas was absent when Jesus first appeared to the apostles at the resurrection. He was a doubter. "Unless I see the scars...I won't believe," he said. Jesus then showed him. Thomas confessed, "My Lord and my God." As a result of Jesus' death, resurrection, and victory, recognition of our own smallness and Jesus' greatness is possible.

Saint Paul, the apostle, shows us another way by speaking of the call to humility and obedience by remembering the humility of our Lord Jesus Christ:

> *Do nothing from selfish ambition or conceit, but in humility regard others as better than yourselves. Let each of you look not to your own interests, but to the interests of others. Let the same mind be in you that was in Christ Jesus, who, though he was in the form of God, did not regard equality with God as something to be exploited, but emptied himself, taking the form of a slave, being born in human likeness. And being found in human form, he humbled himself and became obedient to the point of death — even death on a cross. Therefore God also highly exalted him and gave him the name that is above every name, so that at the name of Jesus every knee should bend, in heaven and on earth and under the earth, and every tongue should confess that Jesus Christ is Lord, to the glory of God the Father.*
>
> *— Philippians 2:3-11 (NRSV)*

In the Bible, Thomas points us to adoration of the Alpha and Omega. So does Paul. How do we move closer to the Alpha and Omega as a personal reality? Consider another story.

A young student once asked the discoverer of the anesthetic property of chloroform, Sir James Simpson, what he considered to be his greatest discovery. This renowned individual, a leader in the field of medical science, quickly replied, "The greatest discovery I ever made was when I realized what sin really was and what a hold it had on me."

"But," said the student, "you've made so many great, positive discoveries; that 'sin' stuff sounds so negative, so discouraging, so depressing." "Oh no, it's just the opposite," said Simpson. "Until I understood how deeply sin affects everything I do; until I understood the coercive, manipulative nature of sin; until I truly understood the depth of it; only then could I begin to understand the freedom, the new life offered by Jesus Christ."

Seeing our sin and Jesus' sacrifice means that we acknowledge him as Lord and God like Thomas and Paul and James Simpson did. They saw their sinfulness, then the salvation of Jesus. Consider another story.

Malcolm Muggeridge, the TV commentator, was a cynic and an atheist. He was converted to Christianity while doing a story on Mother Teresa. He wrote *Jesus Rediscovered*. In it he says:

> *He (Jesus) showed us how to escape from the little dark cell our egos make, so that we may see and hear and understand whereas before, we have been blind and deaf and dumb.*

Consider still another story about the discovery of our sin and the salvation offered by the Alpha and Omega. A tourist who took in the passion play at Oberammergau, Germany, went backstage at the conclusion to meet Mr. Anton Lang, who played the part of Christ. After taking a picture of Anton Lang, the tourist noticed in a corner the great cross which Mr. Lang had carried in the play.

"Here, dear," he said quickly to his wife, "You take my camera. When I lift the cross up on my shoulder, you snap my picture."

Before Mr. Lang could say anything the tourist had stooped down to lift it to his shoulder, but he could not budge it one inch off the floor...the cross was made of heavy iron and oak beams. Puffing with amazement, the man turned to Mr. Lang. "Why, I thought it would be light," he said. "I thought the cross was hollow. Why do you carry a cross that is so terribly heavy?" Mr. Lang replied softly, "Sir, if I did not feel the weight of his cross, I could not play his part."

As we take up the cross of Christ and follow him, we rediscover Jesus, the Alpha and Omega of life — the one from whom we came; the one to whom we go, our Lord and our God. Revelation 1:8 points us to the Alpha and the Omega.

Revelation 1:8 also speaks of the Almighty as the Pantokrator.

The Pantokrator

This word appears seven times in the New Testament. Six of these are in the book of Revelation. It is a favorite term of John, the visionary mystic, who gives us a vision of reality as it is and as it will be. Pantokrator literally means, "the Almighty."

"The Almighty," like "Alpha and the Omega," is an abstract conceptualization. Is there a more concrete way to speak of God, the Pantokrator?

One writer put it this way: "Unless that which is above you controls that which is within you then that which is around you will."

We will make something almighty in our lives. If we don't accept the Alpha and Omega, we will place money, sex, success, or some other person in first place in our lives, only to discover that nothing else works as the Almighty, except God himself.

Consider the story of handicapped children. Having worked some with handicapped children in confirmation, I was deeply impressed by their devotion to our Lord. Their simple acceptance of Jesus as Lord Almighty made me pay more attention to this story.

Most of us have heard about the Special Olympics sponsored by the Joseph P. Kennedy, Jr., Foundation for Handicapped Children, but few know the story told by Jim Murray. Jim Murray, sportswriter for the *Los Angeles Times*, at the time wrote a splendid article about them. He compared what was happening at the Special Olympics with what was happening in Munich at the real Olympics that year. Here's what he wrote:

> *You very quickly learn what is special about the Special Olympics. Nobody was trying to win. There were no false starts and every athlete performed as if he alone were on the track. They ran with a kind of beatific joy. There were no tears from losers. In fact, there were no losers. You take Angie, who ran in one of the lower divisions of the 300-yard run. I use the word ran loosely. You can tell right away that Angie is no runner. An obviously glandular case, her torso is heavy with fat, and it took several seconds for her to clear the starting blocks. She peered down the track in dismay from behind her myopic spectacles. The field was in the home stretch before Angie was properly underway. She lost the race by 200 yards. She stopped several times in some bewilderment at finding herself alone. But from the stands, from her fellow competitors who had already finished, and from her friends, came shouts of encouragement. Then Angie would start up again. About 20 yards from the finish she collapsed happily in the waiting arms of her friends with a wild smile of accomplishment.*
>
> *That's what the Special Olympics are all about. There are stories of the times a winning runner knew a companion had tripped and fallen, and had circled back to help his friend to his feet, costing him a gold medal. There was a boy from Chicago who ran on crutches and a girl who long-jumped on an artificial leg. There was a blind boy who followed the voice of his coach around the track. There was a basketball game without a single intentional foul. There was a boy who finished the race, and then kept running around and*

around the track because it felt so good. Eunice
Kennedy Shriver spoke to the crowd that day. She said
this: The athletes that we remember are not the flaw-
less, but the great human beings who have reached be-
yond themselves to achieve a glorious goal.

Truly great human beings reach beyond themselves. That's what Pantokrator means. God, the Almighty One, causes us to reach beyond ourselves. God, the Omega, pushes us from behind. Pantokrator also means that God leads the way.

Consider this story of Canadian geese:

Have you ever wondered why the Canadian geese fly only in the "V" formation? For years specialists in aerodynamics wondered the same thing. Two engineers calibrated in a wind tunnel what happens in such a "V" formation. Each goose, in flapping his wings, creates an upward lift for the goose that follows. When all the geese do their part in the "V" formation, the whole flock has a 71 percent greater flying range than if each bird flew alone. Each, then, depends upon the other to get to its destination.

When a goose begins to lay behind, the others "honk" him back into place. We have something important to learn from the geese in a "V" formation.

The church needs to fly in a spiritual "V" formation, following behind the One who is out in front of us, and "honking" one another into steadfastness. We've got to follow the Alpha and fly with the flock as opposed to going it alone.

No stories adequately express what Revelation 1:8 means by the Alpha and Omega and the Pantokrator; but the stories we have shared here show us who is pushing us from behind and who is out before us leading the way, the Alpha and the Omega, the Almighty.

Questions For
Reflection Or Discussion

1. There are several stories in this chapter. They can help us take abstract ideas like "Alpha," "Omega," and "the Almighty" into our lives. Can you think of other stories which help to illustrate how God is out in front of us, or behind us, or over us?

2. In the story of the monk's silent story, the congregation realized through the silent sermon what the cross meant. Have you ever had the realization of what Jesus has done for us by his wounds on the cross? What were the circumstances?

3. What can we learn from handicapped children in the Special Olympics?

14

I Am Coming Soon

See, I am coming soon... — Revelation 22:12 (NRSV)

Clyde Schmidt was a member of First Lutheran Church. His family had belonged there for four generations. His grandfather was a Lutheran minister. Clyde and his wife, Ida Mae, were pillars at First Lutheran.

Clyde's faith was shaken one day when Ida Mae asked him for a divorce. It had been a difficult year. His lumber business was quite demanding. He had not spent as much time with his wife and children as he had desired. In addition, Clyde's responsibilities as a church council member had increased considerably since the senior pastor had resigned to move to another community. Clyde was under severe stress. When it was revealed that Ida Mae had had an affair with another man, Clyde's stress "went off the charts" as his friend, Fred, said.

Clyde had tried to be a good Christian leader, a good business man, and a good husband and father. Now he felt like a complete failure. Does Jesus' promise, "I am coming soon..." have anything to do with Clyde's life?

Does the second coming of Christ have anything to say to Ida Mae's adultery? What difference does this obscure verse from Revelation have to do with Ida Mae?

The children, Sara (7) and Johnny (9), are being seriously affected by the lack of communication and the breakup of the family life as they have known it. What does Jesus, the Great I AM who is coming soon, have to do with the feeling on the part of the children that they are the cause of this divorce? Children of divorced parents often feel that if they had only behaved better Mommy and Daddy would not have gotten a divorce.

Before we look at the meaning of the second coming of Christ for the Schmidt family, we should look at the first coming of Christ — his birth at Bethlehem.

The First Coming Of Jesus

Johnny had played a shepherd in the Sunday school Christmas play at First Lutheran a year earlier. Sara had played the part of Mary, the mother of Jesus. Clyde and Ida Mae were proud of their children. The assistant pastor at First Lutheran was proud of them, too. The Rev. Jim Brooker had been at First Lutheran for four years. He had gone there as his first charge, right out of seminary. He particularly liked the Schmidt children. He blessed them at the communion rail. He called them by name when he saw them in the church hallway. After the Christmas play a year ago, he had made it a point to tell them what a good job they had done.

Before a council meeting at which the leaders were talking about the process of getting a new senior pastor, Clyde asked Jim for "a few minutes to talk about something personal." "Sure," Jim said, wondering what it was that Clyde wanted to talk to him about. "Maybe it's about the lumber yard," Jim thought.

As the two men walked to Clyde's car after the council meeting, Clyde said in a broken voice, "Ida Mae has asked me for a divorce." Jim was shocked. He was more shocked when Clyde said, "There's another man involved." Ida Mae was one of Jim's Sunday School teachers. He could not imagine that she was committing adultery. "It just doesn't seem possible," he said.

The two men talked for two hours in the car that night. Clyde had always seemed so much in control, so confident, so strong. On that night, he cried for the first time in years. Jim cried too. "Maybe it's my fault," Clyde said. "This last year I haven't given Ida Mae the attention she needs." The two Christian men prayed together before they left one another at midnight.

When Clyde got home, Ida Mae was still awake. "I've told Pastor Jim what you said yesterday. He said that he would be

114

willing to see you tomorrow." "I don't know," Ida Mae said. "I've made up my mind." "It's only fair that we should try counseling before we take this kind of drastic move," Clyde countered. Reluctantly, Ida Mae talked to Pastor Jim the next day.

"It boils down to this," she told the pastor. "Clyde has neglected my needs for over two years now. He takes me for granted. He doesn't really listen." The pastor and parishioner talked for over two hours. When Ida Mae left, Jim thought to himself, "What difference does my sermon for the first Sunday in Advent make for the Schmidts?"

Jim preached that Sunday on the coming Christmas event. In his sermon, he said, "Jesus descended from heaven to earth so that we would know that nothing we experience is unknown to him. Anything you have ever gone through and anything you ever will go through is personally experienced by him. Before it hits you, suffering hits him. That's the meaning of the incarnation, God taking on flesh."

That Sunday night, Clyde called Jim at home. "That sermon really helped me," he said. "So did our talk last Tuesday night. I'm still hurting from Ida Mae's desire to divorce me, but I don't feel as much alone as I did."

When Pastor Jim met with Clyde and Ida Mae at their house the next day, he asked each of them to tell their side of the story. "Jim has been away too much," Ida Mae said. "When I tell him my problems, he tries to give me the answers instead of just listening to me." Clyde said, "I don't think that there is any hope for our marriage. Even if Ida Mae says that she is sorry, I'm not sure that I can forgive her for committing adultery." The plot got thicker when Ida Mae revealed that "the other man" was Pastor Jones, Jim's former supervisor, the senior pastor at First Lutheran. "I went to him for counseling and one thing just led to another," she said. Clyde was furious. "How could a pastor do such a thing?" he screamed.

As Jim prepared his sermon for the second Sunday in Advent on the second coming of Christ, he pondered the text, "I am coming soon..." (Revelation 22:12), in the light of the stressful situation of a fellow pastor's sexual involvement with the young wife of Clyde Schmidt.

The Second Coming Of Christ

"As Jesus as Savior came identifying with our problems and burdens in his first coming," he said, "Christ will come as Lord with power and justice in his second coming. The meaning of the second coming of Christ is that he is Lord of all and over all. We can submit our lives to Jesus as Lord," Jim said. The sermon seemed to have little effect on the Schmidt's marriage problem.

Twelve years later, as the Rev. James Brooker presided at the marriage of 19-year-old Sara Schmidt, he wondered, "What really happened to Clyde and Ida Mae?" Jim had counseled with Clyde and Ida Mae for six months, seeming to get nowhere. He had left First Lutheran and become the senior pastor of another church in a nearby town. The former senior pastor of First Lutheran had divorced his wife and left the ministry. In his counseling sessions with young Sara, Jim had inquired about her mother and father. "They are still together," Sara said. "They had a 'rocky year' when I was seven, but they got through it. They will be at the rehearsal dinner. You can ask them what happened."

It was quite a reunion when the pastor and the Schmidts met again. After the rehearsal dinner they went over for a cup of coffee at a nearby restaurant. "What happened twelve years ago?" Jim asked. "Can you tell me?"

Ida Mae responded first. "The affair with Pastor Joe Jones broke off shortly after you left town. I was very angry with him and very angry with Clyde. Mostly, I was angry with myself for falling into the trap of letting Joe take advantage of my vulnerability. For me the turn came when Clyde said that he was willing to forgive me and start again."

"My pride was hurt," Clyde said. "My manhood was challenged when I found out about Ida and Joe. I felt like I wanted to kill him. For me the turn came when I stopped being a cultural Christian and really concentrated on being a disciple of Jesus Christ. I told Ida that I needed her forgiveness as well as she needed my forgiveness. It was the hardest thing in my life," he said, "but it was the best thing I ever did. I kept asking Jesus, the Lord, to guide me. Until that period in my life, I had tried to remain in control. It was like I was holding the push-button control panel for a television and changing stations as I willed to do so. The turning point was when I gave up control to Jesus as Lord."

The three Christians bumped coffee cups and toasted the new-found love which Ida and Clyde had discovered. None of them could remember exactly what Jim had said to them in his counseling or in his sermons, but Clyde and Ida told Jim that he had really helped them by just being there and listening. Both thanked him for his continual presence through the toughest part of their married life, and for his guidance and help for the children. "That's why Sara wanted you to marry her," Ida said. "You stood by her when we had our troubles."

As Jim was saying "goodnight" at his car, Clyde asked him for a favor. "Would you preside at our 25th wedding anniversary next month?" he asked. "We want to repeat our vows before you."

At the 25th wedding anniversary celebration of Clyde and Ida Schmidt, Jim presided and preached a short sermon on the text, "I am coming soon..." "Jesus presides as Lord at this marriage celebration," Jim said. The congregation of family and friends at First Lutheran smiled at the strange selection of Revelation 22:12 for this renewal of vows ceremony. "It's the second Sunday in Advent," Jim said with a twinkle in his eye. "The second coming of Christ means that he alone is Lord and that a good Christian marriage is founded on the rock-like foundation of Jesus' lordship." The friends and family of Clyde and Ida did not know any of the details of what had happened 12 years earlier, but they smiled politely during the ceremony. Clyde and Ida Mae wept tears of joy.

Questions For
Reflection Or Discussion

1. Do you know of marriage troubles which have been resolved by a renewed dedication to Christ by both parties?

2. Do you know of marriages which have broken up, even when both participants had faith?

3. Why is forgiveness so important in this story?

4. What difference does the first coming of Christ as Savior make for marriage relationships?

5. What difference does the second coming of Christ as Lord make for marriage relationships?

6. What difference does Christ as Savior and Lord make for divorced persons in our churches?

Epilogue

The story of Clyde and Ida Mae Schmidt is a true story. So are the other stories in this book. Only the names and places have been changed to protect the people involved. Not every marriage is saved by a faith renewal, but my experience is that many can be saved when both parties see a need for Jesus as forgiving Savior and Lord of life.

Using modern stories throughout this book is an attempt to get at Scripture through "the back door." Just explaining the I AM sayings of the Bible may be helpful to some. Trying to find real life applications of these I AM texts may help others as it has helped me. I hope that this book has helped you, the reader.

There are two questions I have asked about every Bible verse: Is it true, and does it make a difference?

I believe that all of the Bible verses used here are true, but if they don't touch us "where we live," they won't make a difference. Using stories is a good way to get at the second question about how Scripture can make a real difference in our lives.

In 1954 I was converted to Christianity by reading a book, *The Greatest Story Ever Told*, by Fulton Ousler. It is my hope that this book will be of help to someone who needs to discover or rediscover Jesus as Savior and Lord of Life. Perhaps someone will meet the Great I AM by reading this book.

The Great I AM is not a dead doctrinal conceptualization. The Great I AM is the living God.